rock philosophy: meditations on art and desire

Torgeir Fjeld

Series in Philosophy

Copyright © 2019 Vernon Press, an imprint of Vernon Art and Science Inc, on behalf of the author.

All rights reserved. No part of this publication may be reproduced, stored in a retrieval system, or transmitted in any form or by any means, electronic, mechanical, photocopying, recording, or otherwise, without the prior permission of Vernon Art and Science Inc.

www.vernonpress.com

In the Americas:	In the rest of the world:
Vernon Press	Vernon Press
1000 N West Street,	C/Sancti Espiritu 17,
Suite 1200, Wilmington,	Malaga, 29006
Delaware 19801	Spain
United States	

Series in Philosophy

Library of Congress Control Number: 2018950574

ISBN: 978-1-62273-708-6

Also available:

Hardback: 978-1-62273-441-2

E-book: 978-1-62273-596-9

Author's drawing on the back cover by Pat Fjeld (c), used by permission.

Product and company names mentioned in this work are the trademarks of their respective owners. While every care has been taken in preparing this work, neither the authors nor Vernon Art and Science Inc. may be held responsible for any loss or damage caused or alleged to be caused directly or indirectly by the information contained in it.

Every effort has been made to trace all copyright holders, but if any have been inadvertently overlooked the publisher will be pleased to include any necessary credits in any subsequent reprint or edition.

Abstract

Is creation an outburst that is not entirely sensible, or is it an eruption that lights up the universe? The relation between creativity and reason made Plato condemn the arts, while others have hailed the spark that uncovers hidden truths. This volume connects thinking about Being, reason, desire and the arts in ways that enable us to imagine how we can be brought into the nearness of truth.

Calls to subordinate arts to reason and tradition have been countered by thinkers and artists that have argued for artistic autonomy. In recent conceptual art this claim for sovereignty has gone even further, attempting to subsume philosophical matters within the creative domain. This current culminates in a vexing question: when art is permeated by purely intellectual concerns, so that the very boundary between philosophy and the arts dissolves, is all that remains of the artwork *as art* an abstract howl of the rock itself?

The abstraction we find in contemporary arts has a precise correlate in the way analysis of desire *in* art ends in a purely mathematical event where desire returns without enjoyment. If it was such an experience of truth and Being Socrates cried out against, his trial was an accusation against philosophy itself. In Plato's writing Socrates would be offered up in ironic and evasive manoeuvres, so that truth was realised by means of negation. On the other side stands John, he who could finally only render Christ through silence.

Keywords: Being, arts, *Gelassenheit*, desire, philosophy

The artwork in chapter 4 is used with courtesy of Olafur Eliasson, neugerriemschneider, Berlin; and Tanya Bonakdar Gallery, New York; and Sigurður Gudmundsson, i8 Gallery, Reykjavik, and Galerie van Gelder, Amsterdam.

© Torgeir Fjeld 2018

...la felicità umana non possa consistere se non se nella immaginazione e nelle illusioni.

Giacomo Leopardi, *Zibaldone*

Table of contents

List of Figures — ix

A Manifesto to Rock Philosophy — xi

Introduction: Thinking, knowing, writing — xiii

Chapter 1	**Volcanic origins**	1
	Plato and inspiration	3
	The flash of insight: Heraclitus	4
	Parmenides and the demand of the phallus	9
	Into the volcano: Empedocles and Ulven	14
Chapter 2	**The time of the rock**	23
	Hegel and nomadic time	25
	Time of the commodity	32
	The becoming of no-time	36
Chapter 3	**Knowing the rock**	43
	Truth and psychoanalysis	45
	The advent and the gift	50
	Perception and forgetting	56
Chapter 4	**The art of the rock**	61
	Reason, freedom and the Absolute	62
	The specificity of poetry: Miłosz and Ulven	67
	Conceptual art and the return to philosophy	75
Chapter 5	**Particles and universals**	81
	Across the multiverse	82
	Passages	88
	The Other silence	97

Afterword: Outside the rock	*103*
Bibliography	*113*
Index	*119*

List of Figures

Figure 1.1: Torus - A torus generated by revolving a circle in three-dimensional space about an axis coplanar with the circle.   13

Figure 1.2: Dualism - Dualisms in Heraclitus, Freud and Lacan.   15

Figure 1.3: Fourfolds - Fourfolds in Empedocles and Heidegger.   16

Figure 2.1: Mirror stage - Phases of Lacan's mirror stage   29

Figure 3.1: Triad - Venn diagram of Lacan's triadic typology.   48

Figure 4.1: The Weather Project - Olafur Eliasson, The Weather Project (2003).   76

Figure 4.2: Come back Muse - Sigurður Gudmundsson, "Come back Muse" (2013).   77

Figure 5.1: Schema L - Lacan's Schema L. Note that the terms on the imaginary axis (a and a') are reversed in his seminar on psychosis.   84

Figure 5.2: Distributions - Two ways to spread metric and matter over a manifold of events.   87

A Manifesto to Rock Philosophy

Rock Philosophy – a philosophy *of* the rock: the indeterminacy embedded in this book's name lays open a prepositional ambiguity. Ours is a philosophy that *concerns* the rock; it is *about* the rock and takes the rock as its subject. However, it is also a philosophy that *emerges from* the rock: it comes out of the rock, in much the same manner as the green clad daughter of the Mountain King in Henrik Ibsen's *Peer Gynt* emerged out of and remained *intrinsic to* the rock that had engendered her.

In so far as the rock is the subject of this volume it is the rock that speaks: we are the ones giving it voice. When we regard it as the object of our philosophy we entertain two distinct possibilities. We implicate the rock *both* as an object we hold in our hand – a rock that stimulates our tactile and visual capacities, a rock we can sense, weigh, carry or throw – *and* as the rock we walk on and that we have come to refer to as our home. On the other hand, "rock" as a verb incites us to imagine the power art and poetry have to *rock* philosophy, a ship on a stormy sea, or a tired child that needs sleep.

When we say that it is time to rock philosophy we acknowledge all these senses: this is a philosophy that can be launched as a projectile, and yet it can also provide us with a sense of belonging; it is a philosophy that has been moved by art and poetry, and it can shift the very grounds of our thought; and in the end there is a time for philosophy to close its eyes and avert the light of knowledge. There will be a time to rest and sleep.

This is provisionally a philosophy that is as much about the rock – a rock, any rock, our own rock, our planet – as it is about the shape of a voice engendered and enveloped by our planet: it is essentially an expression of what the 20th century philosopher Martin Heidegger referred to as our thrownness. We are hurled into our lives. There are conditions to our existence that are beyond our grasp and outside our potentiality of control. And yet we are charged with our lives. We do our best to cope with and nurture existence within our capacities. We are limited by the conditions of our making and these conditions are not of our own making. And in the end, our limitations become our project.

It is within these bounds that the present volume is laid down. It is an attempt to provide the grounds for a thinking that acknowledges our acts as formative for our being and as necessary compliments to our non-acts, our meditations and our thinking.

Introduction:
Thinking, knowing, writing

When the poet Tor Ulven asks how it is that we do not speak up, take to the streets, open our eyes, and scream against our misery, his answer is "because I am of rock".[1] There is an indeterminacy in the original that translates only with some effort: is the poet's incapacity due to his departure from rock, or is it because he is composed of rock? If the former is the case, we could say – with an allusion to the Scripture – that his material point of departure carries as a seed within it the shape in which he will arrive: as we are formed out of dust, so we are destined to return as such. If, on the other hand, the poet is *made out of* rock, he is no longer human, or at least not *merely* human. He has become – as Ulven puts it when he describes to a child what it is like to be no longer alive – part of the objects that surround us.

This threefold consideration of the rock is the concern of the present volume. First, the rock is what emerged out of clouds of dust and gas, solidifying into the planet we inhabit. It is the ground on which we walk, and our common reference as habitat and dwelling place. Second, rocks share with us the minimal components of our bodies: atoms, quarks, electrons. We are – in this very concrete sense – made of rock. The dust we arrived from, and to which we shall return, is already part of our very composition. Third, rocks provided us with the first moulds and canvases into which we could carve our words and paint our sentiments. What connects us to our ancestors is a persistent pondering over the conditions of our existence. What does it mean to exist? What are the necessary requirements for a meaningful life? What are the boundaries that separate mortals from that which lies beyond our immediate horizon?

When Ludwig Wittgenstein, in his *Philosophical Investigations*, asks what it is that makes us attribute affects and sentiments to other people, and, to a lesser extent, to animals, but *not* to inanimate objects, such as rocks, his answer brings up questions of the soul. He explains that "only of a living human being and what resembles (behaves like) a living human being can one say: it has sensations; it sees; is blind; hears; is deaf; is conscious or unconscious".[2] What complicates matters is that, while we can say that "I" have certain emotions and thoughts about them, how can we be certain of what we are? In a thought experiment, Wittgenstein asks us to imagine that when we have a

---

[1] Ulven 2001, 272, author's translation.
[2] Wittgenstein 1963, 97 [§281].

certain sensation, we close our eyes and imagine being turned to stone. How do I know, then, "whether I have not turned into a stone?"[3]

If only things that have souls can feel and think, then it seems within the realm of reason to be uncertain with regard to what it is that senses in this case: a rock, a human being, a soul. The so-called *private language* argument in Wittgenstein is as much about to what extent it is possible to claim emotions to be private as it is an examination of the ways in which we ascribe emotions and thoughts to other beings and objects. In so far as reasoning – and particularly the ability to reflect on our own conditions of existence – is what distinguishes human beings from other creatures, it makes sense to say that reason is something we become accustomed to, and as we acquire the ability to reason, we can attend to what is universal: truth, beauty, Being.

In the essay "Building dwelling thinking", Martin Heidegger holds out the prospect of two different kinds of bridges that each traverse a brook. They both bring adjacent banks into being, collect the landscapes on each side of the stream, making a neighbourhood of meadows and landscapes. The water runs its course between the bridge-piers, in quietude or torrents: in either case, the bridge allows for the shifts in weather, covering the stream as it passes under it, only to release it as it reaches the other side.

These two bridges are as if made in different epochs. One bridge is made of rocks: "the old stone bridge's humble brook crossing gives to the harvest waggon its passage from the fields unto the village and carries the lumber cart from the field path to the road".[4] Here, the material of which the bridge is composed is connected to the labour that gives it its use: subsidiary farming, lumbering, villagers travelling to cross a "humble" stream. The other stands against this early modern, archaic or pastoral image. It is a bridge drawn from high modernity: "the highway bridge is tied into the network of long-distance traffic, paced and calculated for maximum yield".[5]

When Heidegger connects these two epochal views of a river crossing, he does so by reference to our mortality: in our lingering or haste across the bridge, we forget that we as mortals bring ourselves before the divinities. This is the work of the bridge: it gathers those who attend to it, whether they think of it or not, before their mortality so that they can give thanks and present themselves.

The bridges are associated with two kinds of thinking: their work of gathering together disparate landscapes, connecting meadows and villages into neighbourhoods, and as cover and guide for the flow of water is turned into a

---

[3] Ibid., 97 [§283].
[4] Heidegger, Building dwelling thinking 2008, 248.
[5] Ibid., 248-249.

Introduction   XV

question of usage, and, in particular, the value that can be associated with its utility when the bridge is no longer an archaic site of agrarian labour, but a sign of high modernity. The landscapes are transformed from fields into cities, tied together not so much by a modest river crossing, as by a highway with an intermittent bridge, and the river, all but forgotten, seems almost out of place in the contemporary scene: it is not part of the network of long-distance traffic – incapable, as it is, of carrying loads of goods or passengers on its waters – and it lies beyond the sphere of computable utility generated by the standardised, automatized domain of maximum efficiency.

The modern bridge and its attendant technological epoch

> is the mark of all thinking that plans and investigates. Such thinking remains calculation even if it neither works with numbers nor uses an adding machine or computer. Calculative thinking computes. It computes ever new, ever more promising and at the same time more economical possibilities. Calculative thinking races from one prospect to the next. Calculative thinking never stops, never collects itself.[6]

In distinction to calculative thinking, Heidegger proposes what he calls "meditative thinking". It is a thinking that concerns itself with meaning, that is disposed to a calling, and that finds itself in the neighbourhood of Being. Our technological epoch, Heidegger claimed, is in flight from thinking: since meditation cannot yield economic profit, it is worthless for conducting current business and practical affairs. The issue, for Heidegger, was how to keep meditative thinking alive.[7]

These bridges and their epochal situation stand for disparate approaches to knowledge and truth. Calculative reasoning has put into use a model of rationality that elevates utility and maximum efficiency as its primary goalposts. What the rational agent of contemporary science gains in calculability and predictability, it relinquishes in human values and matters of the soul. What counts as knowledge are those pieces of information that can be put into use in the computational model of rationality.

As the computer puts to us a claim for ever more digestible bits of information that it can process as knowledge, our two ways of crossing the bridge become ever more disparate. This quest for ever more information, ever more research is assimilable to the psychoanalytic drive: it continues its accumulative project until it reaches its own extinction. This is why knowledge and research occupy a domain that should not be confused with philosophy's: as

---

[6] Heidegger, Discourse on Thinking 1966, 46.
[7] Ibid., 56.

lovers of wisdom, philosophers know the soul, and to know someone is to know when to say no.

Between knowledge and truth stands the phallus. In this sense, the modern bridge that collects vastly disparate landscapes is nothing but our most base linkages wrapped in the latest dress since it feeds our perceived and real needs for gratification. What is done just as well with the bridge of the agrarian epoch is to bring together beings that make meaning, so that they can gather expressions in a common culture. It is this effort to make meaning from our existence, to question the borders that separate us as mortals and our brief glimmer of light from the vast darkness that surrounds us, that gives us distinction as humans.[8] And it is these kinds of interrogations that presents our true being to ourselves. As Schopenhauer noted, this is a being that is indestructible, so that, even as our individuality perishes as we pass away, our true being persists, and it to *this* being that mortals – whether they are cognisant of it or not – bring their being into nearness.

Is there something supernatural about scripts? The ancients thought that those who were able to carve signs into rocks somehow performed a magical rite as they wrote. In the Bible, God speaks through the medium of writing and provides Moses with the tablets on which were written the law for all his followers. In Plato's myth of Thamus, script is rejected as technology on the basis that it would serve to limit the declarative powers of the king, since it would make it possible for his subjects to bring any new command into view of a record.

Written words are something more and different than mere transcriptions of speech. Today, when we are brought in to culture, this entails learning to read and write for most of us, and it is through such a technology that we are able to participate in *universal* culture. In this sense, culture and the languages in which it is communicated, have a life that far extends our very limited temporality, and it is likely to continue long after we have departed. From the perspective of culture, our most base needs are governable. It is when we have *acquired* culture that we are in a position to regard the drive for knowledge as something that must at some point come to an end, so that wisdom and philosophy can affirm its ground.

Where science becomes philosophy is when the transversal is made from *how* we claim something to exist to *what* gives us ground for existence. For instance, in his 1927 paper on the uncertainty that arises from attempts at measuring the position and momentum of sub-atomic particles, Werner Heisenberg notes that in so far as causality means that we are able to make a prediction of the future based on the state of the present, quantum mechan-

---

[8] Nabokov 2000, 5.

ics disproves the theory of causality.[9] As we move beyond the mechanics of measurement – where is a particle located? in what direction and at what speed does it move? etc. – we find that our uncertainty that arises from the aporia in which precision with regard to the *position* of a particle is covariant with a diffuse rendering of its *momentum* is not a *technical* matter, but, as Heisenberg put it, a question of *definition*. In other words, the uncertainty we have with the reading sub-atomic particles is an *ontological* question.

A similar aporia is given by Albert Einstein's notion of spacetime, in which time is reduced to a fourth dimension of space. As we distribute fields of matter and spacetime over a manifold of events, we are faced with renderings that are incommensurable on the literal level. In so far as we allow for volumes that exceed our current Hubble-determined line of vision, we are given to renderings of universes that are governed by statistical measures: in a spacetime where light has not yet reached, we cannot use empirical tools to determine which events have occurred. It is here that we arrive at a notion of the universe in which our rock is embedded that is decidedly mathematical.

If we are in a world that is wholly governed by arithmetic, mathematics, and what the psychoanalyst Jacques Lacan referred to as *mathemes*, are we not in a world where it is the ideal that takes precedence? Plato, our common point of reference both as founder of our philosophical tradition and as a decidedly *idealist* thinker, argued that the limitation of art, and particularly the kind of art that seeks popular appeal, is that it is wholly derivative: while we can say that the shoe-maker relies on the ideal shoe to make his craft, the painter who paints shoes depends on the shoe-makers rendition of this ideal, so that the painter's work is *twice* removed from the sphere of ideals, and thus secondary to craftsmen.

However, against this derision of the artist, there is a passage in the *Symposium* – aptly quoted by Hans Trausil in his introduction to a translation of Rainer Maria Rilke's *Poems* in 1918 – that seems to indicate a different perception of the artist.[10] While we should cherish those who make businesses, families and states, Diotima interjects, is there not *another* kind of creativity involved in the artist's work. Their souls "conceive those things which are proper for soul to conceive and bring forth; and what are those things? Prudence, and virtue in general; and of these the begetters are all the poets and those craftsmen who are styled 'inventors'".[11] In the end, she is able to convince Socrates that "all creation or passage of non-being into being is poetry or making, and the processes

---

[9] Heisenberg 1927, 197.
[10] See Trausil 1918, xiii, Plato, Symposium 1925.
[11] Plato, Symposium 1925, 209a.

of all art are creative; and the masters of arts are all poets or makers". True artists, then, are those who *engender* ideas, turn that which does not yet exist into existence, and admonishes us with visions of wisdom and virtue.

These inscriptions – scientific, artistic, and cosmological – make sense of and give meaning to our existence in distinctly different ways. The rigour of science strives for precision and a relation to the medium of communication that poetic uses of language would find limiting. The way our world is put together according to the cosmological accounts of origin from the earliest times have some striking similarities to our contemporary language of the composition and nature of the universe, even if the apparatuses in which the cosmos is conveyed tend to have attained a much more restrictive standardisation in our technological era.

How we write about our world and the place of the figure of the writer in that world are questions that cannot be entirely disentangled from our conception of the world. Is the world essentially a unity – one, single entity or core that only *appears* to us as a multitude – or is it more like a river, floating, drifting, changing in shapes and substance? Are continuity and change related in a way that positions them homologously to the earth below our feet and the sky above us, so that the most basic components to our existence are not one or two, but four? Such questions have informed cosmological speculation from the beginning of our philosophical tradition.

And their answers continue to elude us. In a little known story by the writer and critic Tor Ulven the cosmological question is set in an underground world. Echoing the story of Empedocles – the philosopher and cosmologist – who is assumed to have thrown himself into the volcano Etna to demonstrate his immortality, Ulven describes a subterranean landscape of tropical islands surrounded by a vast ocean.[12] The centrepiece of the group of islands is the volcano "Turdus Musicus".[13] There are a great many creatures in this world that are unknown to us ordinary mortals. Strangest of all, however, is the effect of a volcanic outburst: as the innards of the planet ushers out through the top of the volcano, it is not lava that pours down the mountain-side, but beautiful birds of all imaginable shapes and colours that fly off in every direction.

---

[12] One of Ulven's first published texts – written when he was 19 and published in the fanzine *Dikt & Datt*'s inaugural issue in 1972 – "Turdus-øyene" [The Islands of Turdus] is a tour de force of surrealist creativity. It was republished by the literary journal *Vinduet* in 1990 (Ulven, Samlede dikt [Collected Poems] 2001, 231-232).

[13] Turdus musicus is the now outdated scientific name for the red-wing bird. It was suppressed by *International Commission on Zoological Nomenclature* in 1895 and replaced by Turdus iliacus. It is a thrush with a red flank, described by Carl von Linné in 1758.

Introduction

This unexpected and completely secretive eruption of imaginary creativity is a picture of what the arts bring to our existence.

This study is composed of five chapters and an afterword. Whether we regard creativity as an outburst that is not entirely sensible, as Plato did, or as an excessive eruption that lights up our universe, as Heraclitus held, the ability to regard the source of knowledge and creation as a symbol is what distinguished advanced religions from its primitive ancestors. The first chapter discusses how the new order of monotheism dissociated natural phenomena from their symbolisation. This emergent order is what psychoanalysis refers to as the *phallic function*: the call for order and love. The sense in which the entirety of Being is *one* is a key to understand Parmenides' poem on nature – one of our oldest extant sources of Western philosophy. A central concern is the question of whether creativity and reason are commensurate. Plato warned that poets and artists are closer to automatons than sensible beings and that their work can be detrimental to the well-being of their audiences.

In chapter two, the time of the rock is our concern. As Benedict Anderson has shown, our common reference to clock and calendar as the ground to determine what time it is was occasioned by the spread of nationalism in the early modern period. Guy Debord is even more derisive in his critique of this notion of temporality. In his view, it is due to the spread of global capitalism and its dependence on standardisation – including the ability to divide time into segments that could be commodified – that unified, irreversible time has become our common denominator. Other temporalities are possible: as Hegel showed, the cycles of agrarian life were conducive to a notion of temporality that emphasised recurrence and prefiguration. In the philosophy of Martin Heidegger, time is intimately associated with a division in our thinking. While calculative thought relies on clock and calendar, meditative thinking brings us into the nearness of Being.

Chapter three interrogates notions of truth, how they relate to meaning and knowledge, and the experience of being in the nearness of truthfulness. In so far as we can say that we are released into truth, this releasement, what Martin Heidegger referred to as *Gelassenheit*, opens up a clearing that enables us to wonder and question. Truth, in this sense, arrives as an uncovering, and it is in the arts and with artists that we find what Wolfgang Schirmacher has called a *hyperperception* of this clearing. What is required of the hyperperceiver is to return to the domain beyond the clearing through an experience of covering and forgetting so as to regain sense and reason.

While Plato held that art should be subordinated to reason, Renaissance writers such as John Dryden argued for a degree of freedom for poetry. Chapter four revisits this debate through its succinct expression in the work of Czesław

Miłosz and Tor Ulven: while the former gave voice to the orderly and ritualised cultural encounters that flourish through institutions and traditions, the latter held that there is no purpose for art outside art itself. The question of whether art has a tradition of its own, or if art is nothing but a particular form of intellectual inquiry becomes acute with a number of conceptual artists from the 1960s: the boundary between art and philosophical concerns melts away, and the artwork itself seems to vanish into thin air, as is the case with some of Robert Barry's projects. Art reduced to its bare minimum culminates in Ulven's reduction of our biological drive to a howl of the rock. In this sense, art elevates our experience into what Hegel referred to as a *sculpted* form, enabling us to encounter the tragic and unavoidable universality that governs our existence.

Is there life "out there" – on other rocks? In infinite space such a prospect is not only possible, but unavoidable. Somewhere in space, we have a twin that we can distinguish from ourselves only at the moment when we make different life-choices. Chapter five shows how a metaphoric approach to the relation between fields and astronomical events envelops the decidability of astrophysics in speech marked by figures that are possible only to subjects of sexuation. At the end of psychoanalysis, there is a passage where the analysand transforms into analyst. The experience is one of anguish and despair: desire manifests itself as events with a mathematical objectivity that is rendered without enjoyment. If it was such a state of affairs that Socrates cried out against in his speech, his death warrant constitutes a murder of philosophy as such. How do we give voice to the end of philosophy? While Plato depicted a hero that could only be shown through negation, John rendered Christ through silence.

In the end, what we are facing is the question of how we are to make meaning of our lives. History has written the last few centuries in the script of nations, and while it is certainly true that nations exist so as to render death, and, by implication, life, meaningful, how, in a more abstract sense, is meaning something that occurs on a non-subjectivised level?

When Wittgenstein asked whether it is false or nonsense to say that a rock has feelings he urged us to ponder what it is to have an emotion, who or what we can consider to have emotions, and how we ascribe emotions to things and people. Through the "private language" argument Wittgenstein arrived at a kind of collective sensorium that reminds us of Hegel's Spirit, and this kind of knowledge is given the precise description in Freud as *events* or, as Wittgenstein would have it, *emotions*, that *do not (yet) have a proper ascription.*

Does it matter whether our interlocutor – the one to whom events happen, or the one who harbours an emotion – is a person or a rock? A soulless object is certainly able to grant meaning to our existence, not in the least when we associate it with archaeological, ritual or even astrophysical knowledge. What

Tor Ulven showed in his poetry was that through art we are able to endure our rock-like context a little longer.

While art can make the rock speak, it is nevertheless true to say that the rock has the potentiality for absolute silence. It is posited at the end of the drive: beyond it there is nothing, there is emptiness itself.

Chapter 1

Volcanic origins

In the beginning there was fog and darkness. Out of a cloud of gas emerged a slowly solidifying object: a rock, hurling through empty space.

This spherical entity wasn't finished at once. While it is believed that there was a singular event that unfolded into what became a division of earth and sky, man and divinity, the precise distinction between these numerous dualisms were altered by geological shifts that shaped the landmass and its surrounding oceans.

One such dualism is the one we find between earthquakes and volcanoes. Georges Bataille noted how the former has a more feminine character – appearing as seismic shudders as the result of large masses of land bouncing against each other – volcanoes are distinctly masculine both in appearance and aetiology.[1] Bursting forth as sudden ruptures of burning lava, volcanoes have the capacity to engender new land, to alter the shape of already existing ground, and to clear away organic material that had found a home where the volcano's outpouring makes its power felt.

What are we to make of volcanic outbursts? Bataille saw them as exterior evidence of an inner life of the planet – an excessive outburst demonstrating an interior that cannot hold. While it certainly is the case that the outpourings of lava characteristic of volcanic activity show the fragility of the planetary crust, it is nevertheless a question whether the distinction between inside and outside has ever been as clear-cut as Bataille presupposed.[2] Consider the numerous wells or the phenomena of quick-sand, permanently threatening to swallow up those who step into it into the interiority of earth itself.

Then there is the assumption in psychoanalysis of equivalence between volcanic outbursts and experiences of loss and powerlessness.[3] In its most dramatic form it takes the shape of what in psychiatric terminology is referred to as passage to the act, which originated as a legal term in France, indicating the moment of psychotic action where the subject moves from catatonic

---

[1] See "The solar anus" (Bataille 1985, 5-9).
[2] To Deleuze, the human subject appears as an outside that's folded in. Deleuze 2006, 81, O'Sullivan 2005.
[3] Wiener 1998, 496-498. Lacan perceived aggressiveness as "an image of corporal dislocation" (Lacan, Aggressiveness in psychoanalysis 2006, 84).

silence to subterranean action.⁴ In the French legal code, a person who acts under such circumstances was exempt from punishment. A paradigmatic case is the scene from the movie *Taxi Driver* where the protagonist returns to mete out what he considers to be a form of divine retribution on those who have abused his young female friend.⁵

Finally, we should take note of a contemporary tendency to make a too quick equation between any manifestation of masculine action and anger. We should remind ourselves of the sometimes very subtle expressions of the will that nevertheless indicate an imposition on the regular flow of events. One such example is from the professional life of the Argentine writer Jorge Luis Borges, who was National Librarian in Buenos Aires. When asked in an interview why there were none of his own works to be found in his personal library he answered that it was a way for the author to make himself felt: "Yes. You won't find a single book of his around me, because I warned him I'm sick and tired. I warned him of the way I feel. I say, well, here's Borges back again. What can I do? Put up with him".⁶ Here, we have an instance where absence constitutes the imposition of authorial will. And yet, the very lack of books by Borges in the library indicates the presence of its head master.

What we have is a situation of indeterminacy: as evidence of a planetary interior, as experience of loss and perceived powerlessness, or as demonstration of the phallic function, volcanic outbursts are complex events that lend themselves to a variety of significations. The meaning we ascribe to these moments can set us apart or gather us together in an assembly: they are at times commensurable and yet conceivably incongruent. What is crucial is to understand the extent to which the indeterminacy of meaning situates us in a position of thought: since it is no longer certain how we should relate signs to events we are put in a place of wonderment, or, in the language of Jacques Derrida, we are at the beginning of philosophy.⁷

---

⁴ Evans 1996, 136-137.
⁵ Scorsese 1976.
⁶ In the interview with Daniel Bourne of *Artful Dodge*, Borges invited the interviewer to inspect his library: "No, at home, come visit in Buenos Aires, I'll show you my library; you won't find a single book of mine [there]. I'm very sure of this – I choose my books. Who am I to find my way into the neighbourhood of Sir Thomas Browne, or of Emerson? I'm nobody" (Bourne 1980).
⁷ For Derrida, "the whole does nothing but begin:" philosophy and history have only beginnings. Robert S. Gall notes that suspending our homogeneous notion of time in such a manner entails an incursion into our very sense of linear temporality, and it is here that we find "the project of philosophy (metaphysics) [since] meaning – the burning desire and obsession of philosophy – entails a wandering from sign to sign, trace to trace, deferring infinitely the presence it desires" (Gall 1994, Derrida, Jacques, The law of genre 1980, 72).

Plato and inspiration

The creative power embodied in the volcano is a concrete manifestation of what Plato referred to as the divine inspiration necessary for art. In the dialogue *Ion* Socrates explains that the creative act should be compared to the magnetic powers of a certain mysterious rock located at Heraclea:

> there is a divinity moving you, like that contained in the stone which Euripides calls a magnet, but which is commonly known as the stone of Heraclea. This stone not only attracts iron rings, but also imparts to them a similar power of attracting other rings; and sometimes you may see a number of pieces of iron and rings suspended from one another so as to form quite a long chain: and all of them derive their power of suspension from the original stone. In like manner the Muse first of all inspires men herself; and from these inspired persons a chain of other persons is suspended, who take the inspiration. For all good poets, epic as well as lyric, compose their beautiful poems not by art, but because they are inspired and possessed.[8]

What we should note is the way the attraction of the Heraclean rock is compared to the power of artistic inspiration. In the same way as a magnet draws to itself iron objects, divine inspiration has a pulling power on poets and artists. We should take particular note of the way the originating power is located in the rock as a natural artefact, and, analogously, in the divine pulling power of the muses. When an iron object is drawn to the rock – and an artist is enveloped in divine inspiration – it is imbued with some of the originating force so that it takes on a rôle in direct subordination to the primary agent.

As other objects and artists as drawn to an earlier link in the chain of attraction, long series of objects and artists are formed, but in all cases, each element in the series can be referred back to the originating cause: the magnetic rock and divine source of inspiration. In other words, what we have is a case where the artistic outpouring of creativity finds its source in a divine origin, which is strictly analogous to the rock itself.

Already here the theme that has become a topic of much debate arrives as a seed: if the attraction of objects is at its most authentic to be located in the Heraclean rock, so is the inspiration that lies at the core of creativity to be found in the Muse. Those artists that are most intimate with the Muse are those who inspire other artists, and a vein similar to those objects that lie closest to the stone of Heraclea: they become magnetised in a way that makes

---

[8] Plato, Ion 1892, 501-502.

them resemble the stone itself. However – and this is the point that reoccurs with much greater force in Plato's *Republic* – it is the Heraclean rock, and, by analogy, the Muse, that is the *origin* of attraction and inspiration, and all other forms of gravity and artful creation is derived and secondary.

Later, Plato will assert that he who imitates has neither insight into nor a correct notion of the perfections or lack thereof in the things he imitates, and this is why he who imitates "will no more have true opinion than he will have knowledge about the goodness or badness of his imitations".[9]

Whereas in *The Republic* Plato recommends that art be condemned and excluded from society, in *Ion* he settles with the claim that those who make art do so in a state in which they are not in their right mind:

> And as the Corybantian revellers when they dance are not in their right mind, so the lyric poets are not in their right mind when they are composing their beautiful strains: but when falling under the power of music and metre they are inspired and possessed.[10]

What is clear is that already in *Ion* Plato makes an incontestable distinction between those who apply skills taught to them as artisans or practitioners of a profession and artists. The latter are "inspired and possessed" by the Gods, they are "under the power" of music and metre, they are – as Plato will claim later in *Ion* – "out of [their] senses" and lost to reason. The gravity of this claim becomes apparent when Plato draws out the distinction – or, rather, lack thereof – between the artist and the Muse. It is only after vacating oneself of reason that it is possible to make art, since "there is no invention in him until he has been inspired and is out of his senses, and the mind is no longer in him".

What we have in the artist is a state that excludes reason and accountability. It is precisely this characteristic that makes the creative act into a force that has the potential to undermine the law itself: if creativity is only possible to those who cannot be held accountable for their actions, then artistic creation and legal responsibility turn out to be incommensurable states.

The flash of insight: Heraclitus

Already Heraclitus of Ephesus taught that there is a correlation between the excessive charge – experienced as a flash – and knowledge or insight. In his view the world was made through the creative force of the lightning bolt:

---

[9] Plato, The Republic 1888, 316. See the also the discussion of Plato's view on artistic imitation on page 54.
[10] Plato, Ion 1892, 502.

Volcanic origins

> Lightning rules all [and] the transmutations of fire are, first, the sea; and of the sea, half is earth, and half the lightning flash.[11]

Lightning should not only be understood as a literal phenomenon – as an electrical discharge resulting in visual spectacles in the sky – but also metaphorically. To Heraclitus the sudden flash comes to mean the unexpected insight we sometimes experience: "Man, as a light at night, is lighted and extinguished".[12] This is a precise description of how we live our lives: there are moments when we sense an intense proximity to truth and insight, and as this sense of nearness withers away we retreat into the darkness that preceded this experience.

Is this not strictly analogous to the psychoanalytic notion of the aha-*Erlebnis*? The sudden insight into relations that have been hidden to us can appear as a flash, and yet, upon further examination, shown to be fragile or based on conjecture.

Imagine walking through a room in complete darkness. The room is known to us, but the absence of light leaves us to guess at where the objects – which we know are there – are located. Now, a sudden bolt of lightning would immediately envelop the room and its objects in light and enables us for a moment to see the things that we knew were there all along. Nevertheless, it is a brief and momentary illumination: in the next instance, when the flash has subsided, we are again left wandering in darkness.

It is as if the whole of creation is founded upon this very excessive moment when the force of biological necessity can no longer be contained and spills over into creativity. Freud reminded us that the land where the Jews were to found their state was – according to myth – previously uninhabitable due to a volcanic eruption.[13] Only after the land had been shaped by the overflow of lava emanating from the planetary innards did it become possible to settle and found a state where there previously was only sea and fire. Heraclitus' vision rings true: Out of fire there emerges a sea that is divisible by lightning. In the monotheistic way of looking at the world, the creative force has retreated from its physical manifestation. As Freud noted, with Amenhotep III the divinity was no longer directly associated with the sun as the source of life and regeneration, but instead considered as a power that had the sun as appearance.[14] This novel form of *symbolisation* is what Freud used to distinguish between primitive and more advanced religions. While the former transferred the power of knowledge and creation to some physical, visual object – a stone, tree, the sun, etc. – advanced religions

---

[11] Heraclitus 1889, 91 [fr. 28], 89 [fr. 21].
[12] Heraclitus 1889, 103 [fr. 77].
[13] Freud, Moses and Monotheism 1939, 55.
[14] Ibid., 37.

worship a symbol. As the case would be with the Jews, the symbol itself was to be withdrawn and forbidden to articulate. In this manner, the divinity cannot even be uttered from the inception of monotheism.

What is crucial here is to understand the way Freud distinguishes the divinity from any empirical source of light, and the manner by which he makes the distinction possible. When, for Amenhotep III and his followers, the power of creation no longer lies with the actual, visible sun, but with some force that lies behind and guides it, it becomes possible to imagine that there is a kind of knowledge that has its proper place outside the immediate, concrete world of the Egyptians. The abstraction involved in separating the divine power of creation from any physical object in its worshippers immediate surrounding entailed that it became possible to grasp the possibility of a law that existed beyond the physical domain of its subjects. This law – what at this stage appears as a divine law – is what psychoanalysis later comes to name the Law of the Father.

The threefold logic of Heraclitus retained its force in Freud's rendition of the emergence of monotheism. While, for the former, the crucial cosmological event occurred with the transmutation of the sea into land and lightning, to Freud the moment of liquid immersion was absolutely crucial to a whole range of foundational narratives, the story of Moses included. Comparing the Babylonian myth of Sargon with Oedipus and Moses, Freud noted that Sargon, who later became king of Agade and founder of Babylon, was born in secret, hidden in a basket and left drifting in a river, where he was found and brought up by Akki, the drawer of water. As Freud noted,

> The exposure in the basket is clearly a symbolical representation of birth; the basket is the womb, the stream the water at birth. In innumerable dreams the relation of the child to the parents is represented by drawing or saving from the water.[15]

What we have here is an exposure to a planetary component that is *more originary* than the land and those who inhabit it. As we saw with volcanoes as instances of a planetary origin that refuses to enclose itself, the water from the well and the lava from the volcano demonstrate a concrete alignment between the origin of the planet and the beginnings of knowledge. As Heraclitus noted, water is a more primeval state than land, and it is in *this* state that Sargon is immersed and reborn.

---

[15] Ibid., 18. To Otto Rank, "die Aussetzung im Wasser nicht mehr und nicht weniger als den symbolichen Ausdruck der Geburt bedeutet" (Rank 1909, 69, emphasis in the original).

Volcanic origins

While in the Oedipus myth, the child is not immersed in water but left in the wilderness; the effect appears to be similar in that the necessary rebirth can only be brought about as a result of the child's being rescued from a location beyond civilisation and culture. What separates the Oedipus myth from the story of Sargon and, indeed, Moses, is that according to the sources Oedipus was born into a noble family and then reinscribed into civilisation by another royal household. In the case of Sargon, the child was born into modest circumstances, and this is the common circumstance in the set of myths Freud, following Otto Rank, named exposure myths.[16]

In the myth of Moses, the child is born into modest circumstances, but brought up into the royal family of Egypt as the son of the princess. What is unclear is the role of the Pharaoh in Moses' childhood. As Freud noted, there is a version of the myth where the ruler

> had been warned by a prophetic dream that his daughter's son would become a danger to him and his kingdom. This is why he has the child delivered to the waters of the Nile shortly after his birth. But the child is saved by Jewish people and brought up as their own.[17]

This version resonates well with the Christian myth of Jesus, where the prophet is considered a threat to the governing king Herod, who issues a command to murder all children of the relevant age in the kingdom so as to avert the threat.

The theme that runs through all the three foundational myths – Sargon, Oedipus and Moses – is the initial immersion or dislocation of the child in response to a paternal attempt on his life. In each case, the threat is real, in the sense that only a resettlement of the child can shield it from the vengeful force of his father. However, what is also the case is that in each myth the child grows up with an adoptive father, which makes the initial attempt on the hero's life recede into a distant and foggy past. What remain of the initial threat is fear, and it is *this* fear that psychoanalysis today refers to as fear of castration.

The topic of dislocation or, as Freud would have it, *immersion* brings to the fore the order of elements in Heraclitus' cosmology. While the stream and wilderness are representative of the water at birth, there is in these three myths a curious origin in a land that lies *before* immersion. In most cases, children are born, so to speak, from water and brought into protective care on solid ground, in these immersion myths there is a parentage that *precedes* the

---

[16] The term designates the way in which the child would be exposed to water, on occasion in a basket (Freud, Moses and Monotheism 1939, 16-23).
[17] Ibid., 20.

liquid element of re-birth. What we should ask is how this moment constitutes a prehistory of civilisation.

Freud was well aware of the analogies between a man's growth from infancy to maturity and mankind's change from immersion in primitive culture to modern civilisation. In *Totem and Taboo,* he showed the universal preponderance of the theme present in the Oedipus myth, and how the taboo of incest constitutes a common cultural denominator, to the extent that we could say that the theme of this myth is constitutive of culture itself.[18] However, to the extent that the three foundational myths of Sargon, Oedipus and Moses are *immersive* they add another level to the theme of incest and patricide. In each of these three narratives the link between the prehistory of paternal violence and a present of restitution is absolutely necessary for the logic of the story to have its effect: only as the result of an initial attempt at the child's life does it make sense that he is empowered to return and reclaim a position that was rightfully his all along.

It is in *this* sense that we should consider the possibility that there really is *no* change in the level of dominance in these foundational stories: what has happened is an aberration, a non-event. Sargon, Oedipus and Moses were *supposed* to become rulers of their people and the immersion or dislocation made for a dramatic break in a lineage that could nevertheless not be broken. The change or modification posited by the myths turn out to be inconsequential: the seat Sargon, Oedipus and Moses was supposed to take was ready for them all along. The drama appears to exist solely at the level of narrative, while in reality there has been no change.

Here we should approach some of Heraclitus' more mysterious and profound fragments. While his philosophy has often been portrayed as the quintessential articulation of *change* as the underlying force of the universe (everything is fire, fire is the origin of all things, life is in flux like a river, and so on), we could equally well take the view that his is a philosophy of stability and essence.[19]

Critiquing the admonition in which Hesiod was held by his contemporaries, Heraclitus noted that he (Hesiod) was ignorant in one important matter: he

---

[18] Freud, Totem and Taboo 1918. To Lévi-Strauss, the structural moment of Oedipus makes its appearance in the sense that "although experience contradicts theory, social life verifies the cosmology by its similarity to the structure. Hence cosmology is true" (The structural study of myth 1955, 434). The extent to which Freud's reading of Oedipus has become part of the myth itself is illustrated by Lévi-Strauss' remark that "Freud himself should be included among the recorded versions of the Oedipus myth on a par with earlier and seemingly more 'authentic' versions" (ibid., 435).
[19] See, e.g.: "Into the same river we both step and do not step. We both are and are not" (Heraclitus 1889, 104 [fr. 81]).

was unaware that day and night are inseparable.[20] Later, in fragment 36, he goes on to state that "God is day and night, winter and summer, war and peace, plenty and want". In fragment 57 he goes on to claim that "good and evil are the same".

What is so striking about these passages it precisely that they seem to counter the notion of Heraclitus as the philosopher of change and multiplicity. Here day and night are inseparable; the divinity is inclusive of all times of day, all seasons of the year, and all conditions of mankind; and there is, in the end, no clear distinction between what we generally hold to be good and evil. What we have is a kind of universal singularity in which there is no distinction between orders, states or values.

We should keep in mind that even Heraclitus' most celebrated dictum – generally held to be the utmost expression of change as the fundamental condition of the universe – is more complex than a simple celebration of flux and difference: fragment 41 states that "into the same river you could not step twice, for other and still other waters are flowing".[21]

Even Plato interprets this as demonstrating a cosmology of change. In *Cratylus* he has Socrates declare that Heraclitus perceived "that all things flow and nothing stands; with them the pushing principle [othoun] is the cause and ruling power of all things, and is therefore rightly called *osia*".[22] The notion that all things are in motion appear to become contradictory if we accept that motion includes the point of perception: if the position of the perceiver changes at the same rate as the objects that are perceived, then we would have a cosmos that would appear as constant and unchanging from all possible vantage points.

In short, even if change and motion seem on the surface to constitute the essential mode of being to Heraclitus, on close inspection it turns out that there is a constancy and indivisibility at the core of his world-view. It is in *this* precise sense that the world of Heraclitus begins to resemble that of the pre-Socratics most often associated with permanence and stability: Parmenides.

Parmenides and the demand of the phallus

Parmenides poem on the nature of cosmos prefigures the Mosaic theme of a divinity that has withdrawn from the world. Here, it is only by passing through the gates of "avenging Justice" that the narrator is granted access to the domain of truth. In other words, what stands *between* the world of our ordinary sense experience and truth is a moral-legal realm. It is when we

---

[20] Ibid., 92 [fr. 35].
[21] Ibid., 94 [fr. 41].
[22] Plato, Cratylus 1892.

arrive on the other side of justice that we are able to take part in the perspective of truth, which is distinctively different from that of mere "mortals".[23] What is true is that which is eternal: indivisible, immovable and unchanging. If something exists, it has always existed and will always exist. In Parmenides' view, it is an aberration to claim that change is possible. If that were the case, something that did not exist would have to come into being, and that would run against the truth held by the Goddess of the poem: the sense that everything that exists cannot *but* exist.

There are three ways in which Parmenides' view of the world intervenes in our current ontological questioning. First, the location of truth beyond sense experience and finitude indicates that the kind of knowledge Parmenides held in the highest esteem was not to be confused with what we today would regard as sense data or empirical facts. Our senses can deceive us. The only true perspective is that which goes beyond any particular or finite vantage point.

Second, there is a singularity in Parmenides that can only serve to evoke the notion of the Father. It insists on Being, in much the same way as the Law demands its reckoning.[24] In the perspective of Jacques Lacan, there is a lack of Being both in the subject and the Other – which is another name for the law-issuing instance or the Father – that can only be satisfied through an articulation in which the acting subject seeks recognition from the Other. Lacan noted that the element that

> is thus given to the Other to fill, and which is strictly that which it does not have, since it, too, lacks being, is what is called love, but it is also hate and ignorance.[25]

The demand of the Other is that which is excessive of any actual need in the subject, so that the term *desire* comes to indicate the discrepancy between (biological) need and (psychoanalytic) demand. The phallic function is thus the work of the Other in cutting off the subject from its need, or, to put it in

---

[23] The wanderer is held back from ways of enquiry "upon which mortals knowing nought wander in two minds; for / hesitation guides the wandering thought in their breasts, so that / they are borne along stupefied like men deaf and blind" (Parmenides 1908, 198 [VI 5-8], 197 [I 28-30], 200 [VIII 38-41], 201 [VIII 51-54, VIII 60-61]).
[24] Véronique Voruz notes that "a feminine solution seems to imply a different relation to lack, accepting the absence of unification, or one-ification, under the auspices of the signifier" (Voruz 2007, 176).
[25] Bowie 1991, 136-137, Lacan, The direction of the treatment and the principles of its power 2006, 524.

Volcanic origins

simpler terms, it is the moment when the Father says "No".[26] The phallus is therefore different from and more culturally embedded than the penis as a bodily organ. In Freud, the phallus served as a phase that intervened between the oral and anal phases on the one hand, and a fully-fledged genital development on the other. Lacan expanded the psychoanalytic rôle of the phallus to include its position as the key signifier in all of our cultural history, as well as in a synchronic perspective on communication. In Lacan, the phallus has a critical rôle in generating meaning, as it is both

> what sticks out most in the real of sexual copulation, and also the most symbolic in the literal (typographical) sense of the term, since it is equivalent there to the (logical) copula. It might also be said that, by virtue of its turgidity, it is the image of the vital flow as it is transmitted to generation.[27]

The link between sex and logic is complemented by a subtle shift whereby the generative ability of the penis is transferred onto the phallus as cultural icon. The phallic function, then, serves to realign the subject with the order of the Other. However, the price that is paid for this service is an incontestable source of anxiety, since it cannot, finally, be fully redeemed. Lacan pointed out that

> demand evokes the want-to-be under the three figures of the nothing that constitutes the basis of the demand for love, of the hate that even denies the other's being, and of the unspeakable element in that which is unknown in its request.[28]

In this sense, demand presupposes a lack of being, and its claim is constituted as a call that can never be fully answered. The Other exists in so far as it functions as an *instance* in our psychic economy, and a fully symbolised Other would no longer be able to fill this rôle.

Third, the distinction Parmenides foregrounded between the truth of mortals – which has no substance to it – and the indestructible and unchanging

---

[26] This is the notion of the *non-de-Pére* as distinct from the *nom-de-Pére* in Lacan. While the latter signifies the Father as structure, i.e., the Other, the former is the moment when the Other intervenes, which is to say the moment of castration.
[27] Bowie 1991, 124-125, Lacan, The signification of the phallus 2006, 581.
[28] Bowie 1991, 137, Lacan, The direction of the treatment and the principles of its power 2006, 525. Heidegger considered anxiety to be constitutive of the experience of nothingness in which the subject approaches its own thrownness, i.e., its particularity and its being-in-the-world (Heidegger, What is metaphysics? 2008, 52).

wisdom of the goddess puts into play the temporality of our existence. We are bound by a limit, and this limit is, as Lacan noted,

> death – not as the possible end date of the individual's life, nor as the subject's empirical certainty, but ...as that "possibility which is the subject's ownmost, which is unconditional, unsurpassable, certain, and as such indeterminable" – the subject being understood as defined by his historicity.[29]

This is where we arrive at Lacan's notion of the subject as an entity that is *barred from itself,* what we refer to as the barred subject ($). It is entailed by Heidegger's view of the most crucial remainder of our subjectivity, which is impossible to determine, precisely *because* it is indestructible and unchanging. To put it differently, what is most essential to ourselves remains beyond our reach.

The Father as structure – like that moment which preceded our present birth – comes to serve as the instance that issues our most subjective order, and yet it is a *thing* that has a being, even when it arrives to us as a dead object. To Lacan, "this is the dead person subjectivity takes as its partner in the triad instituted by its mediation in the universal conflict of *Philia*, love, and *Neikos*, strife". This truth, then, properly belongs to a dead person, which nevertheless is a necessary complement to our subject formation. As an ancestral, religious or social figure, the Other arrives as a mediating force between the dualism of love and hate, life and death, land and water.

What is this Other beyond the flash promised by Heraclitus' fragment 21? It is the insight that comes to us momentarily and which carves itself into our imaginary. The flash indicates the connection between the indestructible, eternal meaning heralded by Parmenides and the subjective understanding – what Lacan referred to as the "mortal meaning" – that gives light to our existence. As an excess of force, it is precisely that power which we grant knowledge of ourselves that return as a discharge of energy. In this light, Lacan noted elsewhere, we can discern not only our innermost singularity – which, at any rate, is also our most profound universality – but also our destiny.[30]

The centre around which our speech – which is our tool to access the pipes and chimneys of our consciousness – revolves, relies on the phallic symbol,

---

[29] Lacan, The function and field of speech and language in psychoanalysis 2006, 262.
[30] "Is it your countenance that traces our destiny for us in the fire-scorched tortoise-shell, or your flash that brings forth from an infinite night that slow change in being in the logos of language?" (Laurent 2007, 27, Lacan, The instance of the letter in the unconscious, or reason since Freud 2006, 420).

Volcanic origins

but it is a centre that has its existence beyond language.[31] As Lacan noted, there is a sense in which this peripheral centre of our Being shows that the incongruence of our psychic space is more than a metaphor: it manifests a structure. Lacan posited this in the shape of a three-dimensional torus,

> insofar as a torus' peripheral exteriority and central exteriority constitute but one single region. This schema represents the endless circularity of the dialectical process that occurs when the subject achieves his solitude – whether in the vital ambiguity of immediate desire or in the full assumption of his being-toward-death.[32]

The torus – donut-shaped and fleshy – has no centre (see figure 1.1). In this sense it gives a precise rendition of the empty, or, rather, *barred* subject. It is constituted as equipped with a meaning and destiny that is both singular and universal, and the unspeakable and indeterminable part of his being lies *beyond* that which *can* be symbolised. Our innermost core, then, is outside us, and this is why it makes sense to speak of a subject that is *ex-centric*.

Figure 1.1: Torus - A torus generated by revolving a circle in three-dimensional space about an axis coplanar with the circle.

---

[31] Anna O., one of Freud's patients showed that it was possible to reach some understanding of the psyche through the "talking cure" and what she referred to as "chimney sweeping" (Kittang 1997, 16-17).
[32] Lacan, The function and field of speech and language in psychoanalysis 2006, 264.

To Heidegger "ek-sistence identifies the determination of what man is in the destiny of truth".[33] The ek-centric subject seeks to provide for truth within the domain of thought. It is a question of care: when we are called to think we are asked to sustain truth as a way to further our freedom. The ec-static character of Being asks us for its careful consideration:

> As ek-sisting, man sustains Da-sein [Being-there] in that he takes the *Da*, the clearing of Being, into "care". But Da-sein itself occurs essentially as "thrown". It unfolds essentially in the throw of Being as the fateful sending.[34]

This is why our destiny is always a questioning of this thrownness: as we enter into the domain of speech and truth, there is a giving that takes place, and this donation is a remnant we can never cease to re-pay. The paternal gift is not without consequence: as speaking beings we remain barred from the Real of existence, and it is this barring that characterises Lacan's subject.

Into the volcano: Empedocles and Ulven

Before we return to the volcano, let us take stock of the constellations of psychic landscapes that we have encountered thus far. First, there is a demand of *the one*, which we, with Heidegger, have recognised as a singular universality. Insofar as this is an element that lies beyond symbolic communication, it is founded as a structural event. The graphic representation of this occurrence is the *torus*, which has a centre devoid of symbolisation, and whose peripheral and central exteriorities constitute one single region. It is an image of an order ordained by an unspeakable indeterminacy. To the extent that we consider the instance that institutes the law as an abstract ancestral, religious or social figure, it draws its force from the well of phallus as a symbol of the Real of sexual copulation and regeneration.[35]

---

[33] Heidegger, Letter on Humanism 2008, 156.
[34] Ibid., 157.
[35] What Lacan referred to as *das Ding* is glossed by Slavoj Žižek as "the impossible-real Thing, ... that is, libido itself as the undead object, the "immortal life, or irrepressible life" that "is subtracted from the living being by virtue of the fact that it is subject to the cycle of sexed reproduction" (Žižek, Holding the place 2000, 327, Lacan, The Four Fundamental Concepts of Psycho-Analysis 1977, 198).

Volcanic origins

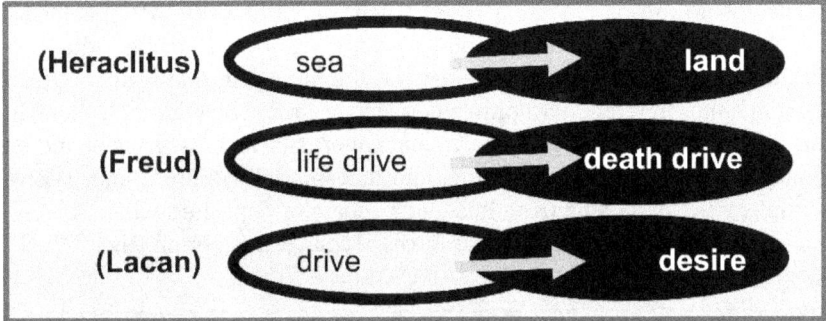

Figure 1.2: Dualism - Dualisms in Heraclitus, Freud and Lacan.

Second, there is the whole range of dualisms encountered already in Heraclitus, who considered that the land which emerged out of the sea should be regarded as a distinct and separate domain of existence. In Freud, there is a recurrent theme of a dualistic formulation of the psychoanalytic drive – which is distinct from the more fundamental biological *need* – most acutely as divisible into life drives and death drives. While the former assisted in supporting and replenishing life, the latter Freud considered as a destructive and dark force. In Lacan the dualism is transferred from a distinction between various forms of the drive – since, to Lacan, all drives are death drives insofar as the key characteristic of the drive is to pursue its own extinction – to an interplay of drives and desire.[36] While drives are desires that seek, but fail, to find their points of satiation, desire relies crucially on symbolic mediation, which can only be activated with the affirmation of the phallic function (see figure 1.2).

This is why desire is always marked by a lack: we can only want that which we do not have, and since there is one love object that we can never have – as it is the exclusive domain of our father – our desire will forever be implicated in our experience of loss and separation. What is necessary for us to begin to articulate our desire is the affirmation of an intervening third: this is the moment Heraclitus referred as the flash, which illuminates the distinction between land and sea, ourselves and our context. In other words, what is enabled through the flash is the Other, i.e., the paternal function.

---

[36] "Each drive ... bears the mark of impossibility: Each is desire seeking and failing to find its point of satiation. Failing to find this point it pursues or half-pursues its own extinction: 'every drive is virtually a death drive'" (Bowie 1991, 162).

There is a third psychic landscape, which was introduced by Empedocles, which is constituted as a supplementary doubling of the Heraclitus' dualism. In Empedocles there are four elements – fire, air, earth and water – which exist in either fraternal harmony or destructive strife. The relation to Heraclitus' notion of a split between earth and water is clearly discernible, and its doubling in a force of change, fire, and its essentially uniform and passive complement, air, enable us to imagine a square of opposites, where the elements of substances are doubled as forces of change and permanence.

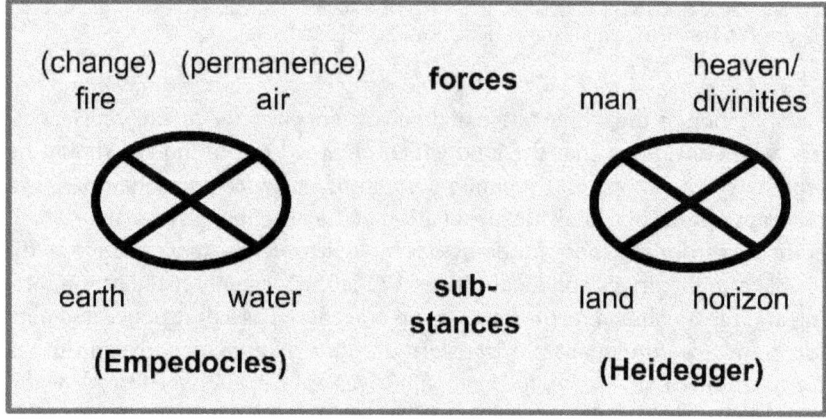

Figure 1.3: Fourfolds - Fourfolds in Empedocles and Heidegger.

In Heidegger, Empedocles' quadrant receives the name of the *fourfold* (see figure 1.3). Here, the distinctions are generated between, on the one hand, the land and the horizon, and, on the other, heaven with its divinities and man. Since there is an interplay at work between the elements of the quadrant, and, in the manner of Parmenides, there is no change to the elements themselves,[37] the circulation and movement in the fourfold provide a ground to

---

[37] "A double tale I'll tell at one time one thing grew to be just one from many, at another many grew from one to be apart" and the cycle of coming together and separation is due to forces of love and strife (Janko 2005, 15). As with Parmenides, Empedocles claimed that these elements or forces neither come to be nor pass away: "Never do they cease from change continual, at one time uniting into one from Love, while at another each is torn apart by hate-filled Strife". While from one perspective it seems as if everything come into being and have only ephemeral existence, from another they "never cease from change continual, in this respect they live forever in a stable cycle".

hold open the possibility of recurrence, or what Heidegger formulated as the moment when "everything returns to itself".[38]

This is what is crucial about the relation between Lacan's Real of sexual reproduction and the eternal recurrence we encounter in Heidegger's formulation: from Empedocles we infer that there can be no outside – i.e., there is no exteriority into which a constitutive element can pass – so that reproduction is what takes place *within* the fourfold. As a consequence, we need to consider whether birth and reproduction constitute anything *new* so that they introduce elements that were not already there prior to the event, or if reproduction instead should be considered as a *reconfiguration* of elements.

These are notions that were present already in the thinking of Empedocles. In one statement quoted by the ancient chronicler, Diogenes Laertius Empedocles, he claims: "Before now I was born a boy and a maid, a bush and a bird, and a dumb fish leaping out of the sea".[39] In this cycle of recurrence and reappearance, there is an element that does not wither, and this is what Empedocles referred to as the soul: "The soul, again, assumes all the various forms of animals and plants".

Recognised by Aristotle as a founder of the discipline of rhetoric, as well as a significant poet and philosopher, Empedocles was considered already by his contemporaries to be in possession of magical abilities.[40] Stories circulated of his healing abilities, and one of these tales include the resurrection of a dead person. Diogenes Laertius recalls how a river that had poisoned a town was purified when Empedocles redirected other, clean streams into it, and so

---

[38] In *Discourse on Thinking*, Heidegger describes our approach to truth as moving towards "something like a region, an enchanted region where everything belonging there returns to that in which it rests" (1966, 65). The notion is possibly drawn from Friedrich Nietzsche's claim concerning eternal recurrence: "How well disposed would you have to become to yourself and to life to crave nothing more fervently than this ultimate eternal confirmation and seal?" (1974, 341).

[39] Diogenes Laertius 1925, 391 [VIII.2, §77].

[40] Diogenes Laertius claims Empedocles was able to master the wind, and so "was called the "wind-stayer" (375 [§60]), and Plutarch notes the common supposition that Empedocles had secured a "whole region roundabout from …pestilence, by closing up the rift of a certain mountain, from whence a contagious southerly damp breathed forth upon the flat of that country" (Plutarch 1909, 424). Pliny the Elder informs us that magic was considered a "branch of science", cherished by philosophers such as Pythagoras, Empedocles, Democritus, and Plato: they "crossed the seas, in order to attain a knowledge thereof, submitting, to speak the truth, more to the evils of exile than to the mere inconveniences of travel. Returning home, it was upon the praises of this art that they expatiated – it was this that they held as one of their grandest mysteries" (Pliny the Elder 1856, 424 [XXX.2]).

made the water good for drinking. When the plague resided, the citizens hailed Empedocles as a God.

There are several claims as to how Empedocles perished. One version holds that he died an old man, perhaps at Peloponnesus. Aristotle was of a close relation view: according to him, Empedocles passed away at the age of sixty. Nevertheless, there are several stories that make quite a different claim, albeit with various inflections to a more dramatic demise. In some of these accounts, Empedocles vanishes during a feast to celebrate one of his magical displays. There is a version in which a number of young women who had no dowry were supported in their marriage by an Empedocles who dressed up in

> a purple robe and over it a golden girdle, as Favorinus relates in his Memorabilia, and again slippers of bronze and a Delphic laurel-wreath. He had thick hair, and a train of boy attendants. He himself was always grave, and kept this gravity of demeanour unshaken. In such sort would he appear in public; when the citizens met him, they recognised in this demeanour the stamp, as it were, of royalty.[41]

What these narratives share is the claim that Empedocles eventually threw himself into the volcano at Mount Etna. According to some historians, Empedocles did this in an attempt to show that he was immortal and thus could not perish.[42] In a further version, Empedocles died by his own hand: the method was hanging.

In any case, the combination of Empedocles view of recurrence and the numerous narratives that revel in a form of *transubstantiation* indicate the fascination with the fourfold that was present already in ancient times. Is it not so, we should ask, if the stories of Empedocles' demise put into play precisely the migration of the soul from one corner of the quadrant to another – from mortal to God and from earth to sky?

One reason why Empedocles are among those mystics and scholars who are assigned to a domain *prior* to philosophic thought proper is not only the kinds of thinking brought into being by his work, but also the *form* his thought is brought down to us. The poetic and narrative structure that shapes the extant record of Parmenides, Heraclitus and Empedocles made it possible for commentators, such as Aristotle and Horace, to compare their work with that of other poets and artists.

---

[41] Diogenes Laertius 1925, 387 [VIII.2, §73].
[42] Ibid., 383 [§69].

Volcanic origins

The boundary between these two areas of engagement with thought and culture is of no small importance, since the distinction shapes our reading and reception of the text. Horace is derisive of Empedocles in the final verses of his letter to the Piso family, claiming that it was flattery that drove Empedocles to the mad act of throwing himself into the volcano. However, Horace entertains the possibility that self-murder would be an act reserved for certain poets and artists:

> Let poets have the right and power to destroy themselves.
>
> Who saves a man against his will does the same as murder him.
>
> Not for the first time has he done this,
>
> nor if he is pulled out will he at once
>
> become a human being and
>
> lay aside his craving for a notable death.[43]

This "craving for a notable death", what Freud later referred as a matter of drive, appears to be a characteristic of some artists, and it seems as if Horace holds open the possibility that there are bards who commit such acts only to return to repeat their folly. The notion of being "pulled out" seems to allude to the question of whether it is one's obligation to take such misconceptions out of the minds of artists who consider killing themselves. But Horace advised against it, on the ground that these are bards who cannot become any wiser or more content, since their pride prevents them from rescinding their fascination with death.

How is it, then, that certain artists fall into this morbid enchantment with death? Flattery, for sure, but the explanation could be more complex. Horace indicates at least two other causes: that their art is of such a nature as to attract morbidity, and that there is some ancestral burden at stake.

> Nor is it very clear how he comes to be a verse-monger.
>
> Has he defiled ancestral ashes
>
> or in sacrilege disturbed a hallowed plot?[44]

---

[43] Horace 1926, 489; cf. 465-469.
[44] Ibid., 469-471.

In the end, Horace saw artists who ended their own lives as cursed, even if it was their privilege to do so. Already in his Roman context, Horace perceived such act to be a reasonable response to profaning the sacred, so that self-murder takes on a distinct hue of a violation of a holy dictum. It is not surprising that Horace completes his letter on aesthetics by declaring such poets insane:

> At any rate he is mad, and, like a bear, if he has had strength to break the confining bars of his cage, he puts learned and unlearned alike to flight by the scourge of his recitals. If he catches a man, he holds him fast and reads him to death – a leech that will not let go the skin, till gorged with blood.[45]

The image of the "baited bear" provides a clear link with the notion of the psychic wound in psychoanalytic thinking. However, on the occasion that such artists manage to break out of their den, they receive power that is otherwise reserved for the transcendental figures of muses. It is after receiving a kind of supernatural force that the "baited bear/bard" pursues learned and unlearned alike before ending his life by his own hand.

Compelling in his supernatural forcefulness and yet repulsive in his morbid fascination the figure of the self-murdering poet received the mark of madman already in the work of Plato. In his dialogue with Ion he made the claim that poets only speak in the absence of thought and reason:

> God takes away the minds of poets, and uses them as his ministers, as he also uses diviners and holy prophets, in order that we who hear them may know them to be speaking not of themselves who utter these priceless words in a state of unconsciousness, but that God himself is the speaker, and that through them he is conversing with us.[46]

Since Plato perceives art to be a property not of technique and learning, but "inspiration and possession" he does not regard artists as skilled, but more closely related to someone overcome with a supernatural, transcendental force that leaves the subject devoid of reason and judgement. This is why the arts are dangerous elements in the state. In *The Republic* Plato held that "all poetical imitations are ruinous to the understanding of the hearers, and that the knowledge of their true nature is the only antidote to them".[47]

---

[45] Ibid., 471-476.
[46] Plato, Ion 1892, 502.
[47] Plato, The Republic 1888, 307.

The balance of reason between philosophy and the arts is therefore decisively tipped in the favour of philosophy in *The Republic*. It is reason that is the tool that can enable readers and listeners not to get seduced by artists and their unconscious ravings.

Chapter 2

The time of the rock

In his important study of nationalism, Benedict Anderson noted the centrality of the *journal* to the invention of the modern nation. Here, he found, lay the seeds to an entirely new imagination – a reconfiguration of spatial objects arranged according to a temporal order that was brought into being through a strict reference to clock and calendar. From the beginning the nation depended as much on the journal as the journal on the nation: the idea that an event could take place in Lima, while *something else* happened in Madrid became a founding conception for a world that was no longer arranged as imperial centres, whose events were reflected and repeated in its colonies, but as serially arranged nations that were considered to be formally equal and inherently limited: beyond each nation there was always *another* nation.

The notion of time measured in terms of clock and calendar, or what Anderson referred to as *homogeneous, empty time*[1], provided its subjects with a view of the world that was distinctly different from the one disseminated by the previous dynastic regimes. There, a sense of prefiguration and fulfilment had governed, such as when the attempt on Isaac's life would be considered as a prefiguration of the slaughtering of the Messiah in the New Testament. The sense we get of a seismic shift in spatio-temporal configurations from the Feudal to the modern, nationalist epoch in Anderson's *Imagined Communities* bears a close resemblance to Mikhail M. Bakhtin's notion of *chronotope*. In this latter formulation literary texts arrive to us with distinct views of the world that entrench themselves as relations of time and space, and of time *to* space, so that while the medieval romance presupposed an unchanging world of shepherds and herdsmen, the 19th century realism of, say, Dickens, sought to convince the reader not only that social change measured along a time scale was *possible*, but that it, indeed, was *desirable*.

The chronotope of the nation, as we find it in journals, newspapers, popular fiction and so on, makes it possible to envision a world with a number of nations that co-exist, and whose temporality conjures events that take place at the *same time* as other nations experience *their* existential moments. Fur-

---

[1] This phrase he borrowed from Walter Benjamin's ground-breaking essay on historiography, "Theses on the philosophy of history" (sometimes referred to as "On the concept of history") (Benjamin 1969 [1940], 253-264).

thermore, these moments may be entirely distinct and unrelated, so that what we have in the modern notion of national time is *not* a sense in which there are events that take place in a centre that are simply reflected or repeated in the periphery, *nor* a presupposition of moments that have been prefigured by some historical event, rendering the present as merely an echo of the past, but a claim to a historical temporality that *does not* repeat itself, i.e., in which every moment is unique and new.

What we have here is a situation where what was *one* entity with an internal hierarchical division – empire and colony – becomes *two* distinct and formally equal units. One divides into two: there is a siphoning off of what was once regarded as part of an empire into a nation, and, as a consequence, the core of the empire itself is reduced to nothing but a nation among nations.

Does this separation not have its correlate in the history of psychoanalysis? In 1938 when Freud was on his way through Europe, on the run from Hitler, he stopped in Paris. Jacques Lacan, who, six years earlier had sent Freud a copy of his doctoral dissertation, was well aware of the master's fleeting visit. Nevertheless, he didn't show up at the train station to greet Freud. The meeting between them was, to borrow a phrase from Derrida, an event that never took place.[2]

To what should be ascribed to Lacan's abstention from this event? Was it due to some eternal duty that intervened? Had he not retained his original interest in Freud as scholar and founder of psychoanalysis? Or was it simply due to a sentiment often recounted in psychoanalytic writing, the fear that can paralyse us in the prospect of an encounter with the Father? If Lacan decided to put off the meeting with Freud because of a more or less unconscious anxiety of what the elder analyst would say or indicate to his younger student, what occurred at the train station in Paris that day in 1938 was nothing short of a re-enactment of the very foundational theme of psychoanalysis itself, Sophoclean moment of modern psychoanalysis.

The event indicates the extent to which Freud's departure from continental Europe marks a split in the body of psychoanalysis and between the custodians of this form of therapy. The most telling signs of such a split are precisely feelings of anxiety and insecurity that arrives in the face of a prospective encounter with the father. It is, after all, the position of that father that is at stake, and such emotions are *indexical* of a splitting of the subject. What we can surmise is that the emerging entity can relate to an ego according to which desire can be imitated and mediatised: someone else has something

---

[2] Derrida, Before the Law 1992, 210.

that we want, and it is this feeling of *lack* that Lacan had already in 1936 described as the experience of primordial jealousy.

Analogously, this experience is common to the division of empires into constituent nations: what a new political unit emerges from under the imperial umbrella, it does so with the assumption of a subject that has a recent experience of division. The effect of the split is that the newly formed nation is in a position to imitate and mediate the desire of its former master. Subsequently, nations of victimhood and oppression of a former imperial master can last a long time after colonial liberation.

Hegel and nomadic time

In *Society of the Spectacle* Guy Debord comments that to Hegel time was a purely formal element in nomadic life, since migration from one place to another did not constitute any significant difference in their subjective experience.[3] As the nomadic tribe followed the natural migration of animals and the seasonal shifts in vegetation, each place would offer food to eat, water to drink, a place to make a dwelling, and so on. It is in this sense that Debord found that nomadic time was marked by repetition: the formal difference in dwelling is annulled by the necessities of the nomadic search for sameness, and, as a consequence, time can only be marked by the cycles of day and night, and the seasonal, repetitive structure. To Debord, "the temporal return to similar places now becomes the pure return of time in the same place". In other words, places return in their repetitive conditions and time is experienced as a pure formality.

Could it be experiences of this kind that made Heraclitus overturn the force of change that had become his signature?[4] In fragment 35, he would declare that the historian Hesiod, while considered a great teacher, "did not know day and night. For they are one". And later, in fragment 36, Heraclitus will claim that "God is day and night, winter and summer, war and peace, plenty and want". This version of the world seems to stand at odds with the notion that Heraclitus held fire and change to be the constituent forces of the world. Instead, there is a unity in day and night, winter and summer, and it is this unity that he will use to refute the teachings of Hesiod.

It is as if *behind* our experience of temporal change there is a universality that remains what it is, and it is this force that Hegel later will refer to as the

---

[3] Debord 1983 [1967], §127.
[4] See the section on Heraclitus on page 14 for a fuller treatment of the themes of change and persistence.

absolute.[5] To Hegel, nomadic experience forecloses participation in the absolute, since there can be no objective history as long as there is no record and no attempt to universalise experiences.

> The periods …that were passed by nations before history was written among them …are on that very account destitute of *objective* history, because they present no *subjective* history, no annals.[6]

It is only with the advent of an enduring record that a universalisable consciousness can arise. Hegel found that it is only with the attainment of an objective existence that this kind of consciousness can arise. Such a substantial matter – "God or Law" – enables the subject to distinguish between "himself as an individual and the universality of his essential being".[7] The resulting knowledge "of an Absolute Being, an Other and a Higher than his individual self" is what enables the subject to participate in objective history.

The coming-into-being of these entities – the universal Being and the individual self-consciousness – indicate a split of the idea itself. To Hegel, the universal Idea had two distinct sides: "the substantial totality of things on the one side, and …the reflection of the mind on itself".[8] This latter notion Hegel determines as the diametrical opposition to Being in its universality, as the individual exists in "absolute Limitation [and] particularisation". As individuals, we have a definite existence that is constituted as a "formal reality" through the "reverence paid to God".

What is clear here is that, first, the individual exists in and through the Other, i.e., God or the Law, and, second, that the individual exists *in so far as* it acknowledges its constitution as a moment in a matrix of power. It is through our reverence, praising and granting of glory to the Other that we continue being granted existence, and it is this relation of dependence that the individual has to the institutive instance of order that consecrates the individual being.

---

[5] In the Introduction to his, *Lectures on the Philosophy of History*, Hegel noted that "consciousness alone is clearness; and is that alone for which God (or any other existence) can be revealed. In its true form – in absolute universality – nothing can be manifested except to consciousness made percipient of it. Freedom is nothing but the recognition and adoption of such universal substantial objects as Right and Law, and the production of a reality that is accordant with them – the State" (Hegel, Lectures on the Philosophy of History 1914, 62).
[6] Ibid., 64.
[7] Ibid., 97.
[8] Ibid., 27.

In other words, what Hegel grants priority in this dual relation is the Universal Idea. The individual emanates as a particularisation and a limiting instance out of the totality of beings and has only a secondary and derived existence. Already here we have a temporality at play: first there is Universality as Idea, and then there is the possibility of the individual as a limiting instance. Is not as if the singularity is granted existence through a *splitting off* from the totality of Being?

It is a question that Hegel could have inferred from George Berkeley's work on perception. In his well-known dictum *esse est percipi*, to be is to be seen, Berkeley captured precisely the primacy of the Universal over and above the individual.[9] To the individual there is existence *only in so far as* it is perceived. This notion of being perceived by others, and, in the final instance, by an Other – God or the Law – is the exact notion that is captured by Hegel later. It is to the mind and perception of the Other that the individual is granted existence, and, even if Hegel emphasised idea and consciousness at the expense of visionary perception, it is a strict analogy between the two notions of the general and universal as primary and originary in relation to singularity and particularity.

These are key ingredients to the formula of individuation in the psychoanalytic thought of Jacques Lacan. Already in his 1936 paper on "The mirror stage" he showed that the child enters into a different kind of relation to the world when he is able to perceive himself and his body *from the outside*. In other words, it is the possibility of an *external gaze* that changes everything in the child's world. This effect, Lacan claimed, can be achieved simply by placing the child in front of a mirror – thence the notion of the stage of mirrors, *stade du miroir* – and allowing the child to experience the change in the visual environment his body is located in when he moves and manipulates his own body, or, more precisely, the child will experience that the visual image of his own body is altered in pace with his own manipulations, while the exterior environment remains unchanged. What remains to be concluded by the child – and the ends through which he achieves consciousness of himself – is that he is able to manipulate his own image: the way he appears to an other is complete and total, and this is a completeness and totality that can be altered and manipulated by the child.

---

[9] "All those bodies which compose the mighty frame of the world, have not any subsistence without a mind, that their being [*esse*] is to be perceived or known; that consequently so long as they are not actually perceived by me, or do not exist in my mind or that of any other created spirit, they must either have no existence at all, *or else subsist in the mind of some Eternal Spirit*" (Berkeley 1874, 197, emphasis added).

This moment is what Lacan referred to as the formation of the *ego*. In his formulation, we are at this intermediary phase of the mirror stage enamoured by our own image, fascinated by the discovery of perceiving our own image in the same way as others do, and the resulting effect is the establishment of a *fictional direction* of the ego. What we have is a sense of ourselves that comes into being in an attempt to satisfy the totality we perceive as our image, and the gap between what we are and what we *would like* to be, becomes the engine of our quest to adjust to the world.

Crucially, this is a moment that ushers into a novel sense of self for the child, and as such it provides a rupture in the child's perception. What we *cannot* say, however, is that the child is now set on a course to discover itself. To Lacan, the narrative consistency of the ego is never complete, in fact, it should rather be considered as a fiction. When the reality rubs up against the frame that the subject has made for itself, it responds with a series of withdrawals and defensive manoeuvres. Thus, drawing on the work of Anna Freud, Lacan compared the ego to a fortress and a stadium. As a defensive structure it is designed to keep out intruders and perceived threats against its foundational frame, and as a stadium it constituted a gaze that is seemingly fixed on *itself*: it is raptured by questions such as *who am I* (in distinction to other individuals), what gets *me* going? and so on.

What the child does not yet comprehend is that this gaze that it has transfixed on itself is not its own. We learn to see and the way we observe is closely managed and supervised. When the child first sees itself in the mirror it is as if there is another instance present. Standing behind the child, it is this presence that points the child to its own image with the words "That is you" – "Thou art that!" This statement is both true and untrue: there is a sense in which the person depicted in the mirror is an individual that is *distinct* from the person imagined as speaking when the child sees itself, and yet is it not so that the fullness of the image is a "you" that the child will never be able to live up to?

It is this distinction that Lacan, following Sigmund Freud, referred to as the difference between the *Ego Ideal* and the *Ideal Ego*. The latter is the instance speaking to the child when the child observes itself: it is the position or figure that the child acts so as to impress. The Ego Ideal is the ideal that we have of ourselves. We often like to think that this is a false image, put into us by some foreign agent. However, to Lacan it is ourselves who conjure this agent: it is the *Ideal Ego*, and it is *this* instance that made it possible for us to imagine ourselves as subjects in the first place.

The time of the rock

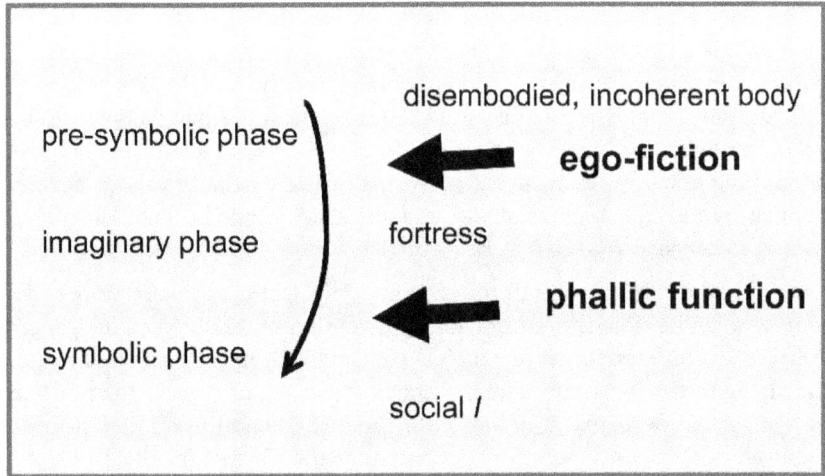

Figure 2.1: Mirror stage - Phases of Lacan's mirror stage

Now, there is a third and final phase of Lacan's mirror stage, and that is the phase in which we can become aware of the difference between the *I* as syntactical/grammatical category and an abstract notion of subjectivity (see figure 2.1). This phase is what Lacan referred to as the *social I*. What is crucial for this phase to incur is the intervention of the Father – what Lacan referred to as the phallic function. It is when we, so to speak, has trailed the Ideal Ego too close, that the father intercepts and draws a line that becomes a legal boundary. In other words, we are removed from the strict position of children and receive the potentiality of rivalry and sexuation.

It is when this latest phase *does not* occur that the subject experiences effects of paranoia: should not the father show his care for us? Should he not instruct us when he has ventured too intimately into his terrain? The refusal of the father is therefore absolutely crucial in order for us to function as sexuated beings, and it is through his intervention – what Lacan on a more general level will refer to as the intervention of the Other – that we can begin to perceive ourselves as subjects.

Lacan's formalization of the coming-into-being of the subject thus has *two* distinct temporal moments: first, the emergence of the *I* out of a disembodied and incoherent pre-symbolic phase, and, second, a transition into the symbolic order, inaugurated by the envelopment of the phallic function. In Hegel's terms, this kind of developmental lineage indicates the possibility of a trajectory that is *cut short* in the nomadic life-world. What we have is an *I* that *does not* transpose itself into a universal category, so that the nomadic subject *remains* individual, without ever reaching the universal.

The non-presence of an Absolute Being – a Law or Hegel's God – to the nomad entailed that this kind of subject would be bereft of the possibility of participating in what Lacan would later refer to as the *social I*. What we have instead is an *I* that is completely attached to itself, and, since there would be no objectification of history, there would also be no subjective history: the nomad remained enclosed in his individual existence, and to move beyond nomadism and its ignorance of laws and universals would be a necessary step to attain a sense of a *social I*.

Freud had a similar point in mind when in his last major work, *Moses and Monotheism*, he noted that prior to the invention of an abstract, allegorical deity, man was abandoned to concrete particulars in his ascription of supra-individual forces.[10] A stone, a tree, or the physical sun could take the position of a supernatural being. It is only with the introduction of an all-powerful, removed and abstract notion of divinity that the Egyptians, and, later, the Jews, could move beyond the particularist notion of the divine and into a universal, and what Hegel would refer as an *objective* position.

This distinction returns in Lacan's use of the terms alienation and separation.[11] As Slavoj Žižek notes, there is a sense in which there is a

> constitutive *alienation* of the subject in the symbolic order: the big Other pulls the strings; the subject does not speak, he "is spoken" by the symbolic structure.

What we are presented with is a notion of order that deprives us of the effects of our acts: we cannot fully determine the outcome of our interventions in the world since the Other is always there to undergird and overtake our determinations. However, there is also a counterpoint to alienation in the work of Lacan, and that is a sense of separation that follows *after* alienation has been overcome:

> alienation *in* the big Other is followed by the separation *from* the big Other. Separation takes place when the subject realises how the big Other is in itself inconsistent, purely virtual, "barred", deprived of the Thing – a fantasy is an attempt to fill out this lack *of the Other, not of the subject*: to (re)constitute the consistency of the big Other.[12]

---

[10] Freud, Moses and Monotheism 1939, 35-41. This theme is developed more fully in the discussion on Freud on page 14.
[11] See Žižek, Holding the place 2000, 327.
[12] Žižek, Da Capo senza Fine 2000, 253.

The time of the rock 31

It is for *these* reasons that it makes sense to say that alienation occurs when we do not experience *enough* lack and deprivation: only when we realise that the Other will never provide us with the sense of fullness and completion we claim to have been alienated from can we fully endorse the division between the subject and the Other, or, to put it in a properly psychoanalytic sense, it is when we step beyond the purely phantasmatic semblance provided by our attachment to an alienation *in* the Other that we can fully realise the extent to which the unconscious is, indeed, the discourse of the Other.[13]

It is in the shift from nomadic, pastoral time to agrarian time that history moves into a notion of repetition that is fully cyclical: it is only then that human history is completely enveloped in the seasonal alterations and their repetitions, Guy Debord found that it is in an agrarian society that we should locate the beginning of labour, since it would no longer be possible to uphold the provisionality and carefree approach to life that a nomadic lifestyle could still support.

> The agrarian economy in general, dominated by the rhythm of the seasons, is the basis for fully constituted cyclical time. Eternity is *internal* to is, it is return of the same here on earth.[14]

Agrarian time made possible settlements and institutions that could maintain records and guarantee a certain continuity, both in matters of Law and governance, but also in the way of mythopoetic provision. The question of *praising* becomes even acuter: Hegel noted that our individual existence is guaranteed only insofar as there is a relation with an Absolute Other, and that this is a relation that needs to be maintained through praising and reverence. With the settled, sedentary lifestyle of the agrarian economy, it became possible to institutionalise this element of consecration, and Debord would emphasise the relation between mythopoetic content and the practice of praising:

> Myth is the unitary construction of the though which guarantees the entire cosmic order surrounding the order which this society has already in fact established within its borders.

The cosmic order provided agrarian society with a notion of eternity – a claim to the Absolute – within which the individual could be constituted. Nevertheless, this relation with the Absolute – the divine order, as it were – would still

---

[13] "The unconscious is the Other's discourse" (Lacan, Seminar on 'The purloined letter' 2006, 10).
[14] Debord 1983 [1967], §127.

be in need of maintenance, and this kind of upkeep is what would later be known as the *sabbatical* aspect of religious practice.

In the Talmud as well as in the New Testament eternal life is what guarantees the provision of a power that is boundless and at rest. The Talmud says that "in the world to come …the just will sit with their crowns on their heads and be refreshed by the splendour of the *shekinah*", i.e., the divine presence. It is this quality of praise that maintains power and allows it to govern with a sense that it governs *for eternity*.[15]

Time of the commodity

It is only with the advent of modernity and arrival of the *commodity* that we can speak of a temporality that is properly linear and what Walter Benjamin would refer to as "empty, homogeneous".[16] Benedict Anderson crucially identifies this notion of time with the ascension of national communities, since it was through the inventions of newspapers and journals, historical novels and stories of conflict that nations came into being.

Debord remarked how cyclical time remained outside conflict and upheaval, and that wars and disasters intruded as foreign and unwanted moments to the cyclical mind-set:

> The owners of historical surplus value [would be] separated from the collective organisation of time which predominates with the repetitive production. …This time flows above its own static community. This is the time of adventure and war, when the masters of the cyclical society travel through their personal histories, and it is also the time which appears in confrontations with foreign communities, in the derangement of the unchangeable order of society.[17]

This kind of disturbance to cyclical time is in Debord's view introduced from above. With the narratives of national communities, such elements would become constitutive of the foundational moment of the nation. Wars of liberation from the imperial centre, stories of national adventures, encounters with other nations, and fundamental upheavals of communities, their beliefs, and the very notion of time itself became key components in the world-view we today recognise as distinctly national and, therefore, global.

---

[15] See Agamben 2011, 247.
[16] Benjamin 1969 [1940], 263-264 [§XVIII].
[17] Debord 1983 [1967], §128.

The interest that undergirds the new national communities is that of what Anderson referred to as the "creole pioneers".[18] These were descendants of the first migrants to the colonies, often successful farmers, traders and merchants, and – later – industrial entrepreneurs, who could nevertheless not get access to the administrative institutions of their society. It had to do with purely imperial ambition: the centres of global domination at the time – Madrid, London, Paris, and so on – would maintain their hold on the colonies by appointing governors in temporary posts. When their time was up, they would be recalled to the crown, and a new candidate would fill the post. It was a means to secure the continued loyalty of the colonial administration.

To those who lived and had made their destinies in the colonies, it was a brutal and unforgiving fact: the empire would never allow anyone born in the colony to ascend the ladder of state privilege. The colony was a reflection of events that took place at the centre of the imperial world, and this centre would remain with the crown for as long as the empire maintained its foothold. What was needed was therefore not simply an overthrow of military and economic dominance by the empire, with an entirely new view of the world, a view in which the colonies did not simply reflect and echo events that had already taken place in Europe, but which had a singularity and the potentiality for *simultaneity* with events that took place in the centre of what would become a former empire. This notion of time is what Anderson, following Walter Benjamin, would refer to as *homogeneous and empty*, since it enabled a world of *simultaneity and cross-transversal*: events in Lima, say, would happen while *other* events took place in Buenos Aires, or, indeed, Madrid. Time would no longer be marked by the religious and agrarian prefiguration and fulfilment (the attempt at Isaac's life would have been imagined as a prefiguration of the murder of Christ, and so on), but as a smooth and even flow that did not have any intrinsic meaning.

With the spread of national communities as the norm for social organisation across the world, the notion of time as measured by clock and calendar has taken the position as the natural sense of temporality. In the place of foundational, religious (or, for that matter, dynastic) events, the nation would situate a heroic past, often separated in an absolute manner from the present, so that those who inhabit the national community could only marvel and admonish the historic spectacle conjured by the national narrative.[19] Anderson's point that the nation exists as a productive force even today is demonstrated by the proliferation of monuments to the (national) *unknown soldier*: this is a figure that embodies the sense in which nations are there not so much to provide us with something to live for, as it gives its subjects something to *die for*.

---

[18] Anderson 2006 [1983], 47-66.
[19] See Bakhtin, Epic and novel 1981, 16.

The novel national community is therefore grounded in its obsession with heroic death and martyrdom. Debord noted how it is an aspect of modernity to posit *irreversible* time (i.e., not marked by cyclical recurrence) accompanied by an obsession with death. To Debord, "this is the melancholy of the demise of the world, the last world where the security of myth still counterpoised history".[20]

The incessant and insistent preoccupation by national communities at establishing a past that is unique and singular therefore rubs up against what Debord referred to as "the demise of the world" of myth. As Bakhtin had shown already in his essay "Epic and novel", national narratives are remarkably similar in some crucial senses: they have founding fathers, heroic moments and – as Anderson would add – make dubious claims to antiquity that could only be questioned with reference to their objective novelty.

When time became homogeneous and empty, measured by clock and calendar, and no longer marked by repetition and cyclical recurrence, it also became *irreversible*. It is this *linearity* that is characteristic of what Debord referred to as the bourgeois notion of time: to them the revolution marked year one, and everything that happened later would have this point in time as an absolute reference – inaccessible, completely separated from the present of the community, and totalising in its signifying capacity – indicating the introduction of a general sort of *freedom*. One should learn to accept that modernity signalled abolishment of the "last remnants of the mythical organisation of values and the entire traditional organisation of society".[21] The novel freedom, even though dressed up in garments of Roman antiquity, was nothing more than "*the freedom of generalised commerce*".

The national revolutions of the late 18th century and onwards *did* bring about an entirely new conception of freedom, both in the sense of national self-governance and as personal liberties, but, and more importantly, it brought about a completely new notion of *time*: as the national kind of community and nation as a source of personal belonging and anchorage became the *norm*, nationalism's temporality manifested itself as global. To Debord, this was the stage when irreversible time became "unified on a world scale:"

> What appears the world over as *the same day* is the time of economic production cut up into equal abstract fragments. Unified irreversible time is the time of the *world market* and, as a corollary, or the world spectacle.[22]

---

[20] Debord 1983 [1967], §138.
[21] Ibid., §144.
[22] Ibid., §144, emphasis in the original.

What is clear is that this novel notion of time became immensely useful in the specialisation of production. With the imposition of substitutable and interchangeable units of production, time would be nothing more than one negotiable entity that could be organised under the general aegis of rational objectification, in other words, time became a market commodity.

Debord would note in the final section on *Time and History* that universal history *would* be possible under this generalised notion of universal time, but the consequence of such an imposition is that of a refusal of history within history itself. What *appears* as a natural, orderly and general notion of time is nothing but the imposition of the world view of a certain interest: "the time officially affirmed over the entire expanse of the globe as the *general time of society* refers only to the specialised interests which constitute it and is no more than a *particular* time".[23]

Walter Benjamin made a point that closely resembles Debord's 25 years earlier, when he, in his well-known "Theses on the philosophy of history", remarked about historical scholarship, that those who measure history with clock and calendar are content

> with establishing a causal connection between various moments in history. But no fact that is a cause is for that very reason historical. It became historical posthumously, as it were, though events that may be separated from it by thousands of years. A historian who takes *this* as his point of departure stops telling the sequence of events like the beads of a rosary. Instead, he grasps the constellation which his own era has formed with a definite earlier one. Thus he establishes a conception of the present as the "time of the now" which is shot through with chips of Messianic time.[24]

What Benjamin advocates is a form of historical truth-telling that enables us to objectify irreversible time itself, in other words, a historical perspective that *allows* for precisely a notion of time that is able to perceive repetition and cyclical recurrence. A time in which the entire history is already present – a temporality that dares us to affirm linearity as but *one*, particularised conception of history – points to an experience of the world that is *not* marked by one moment in succession of another, but where moments are, as it where, *stacked* onto each other and experienced in their full and present complexity. To grasp the implications of such a perspective, it is necessary to move beyond the two forms of time we have considered thus far – cyclical and linear – and attend more closely to

---

[23] Ibid., §145, emphasis in the original.
[24] Benjamin 1969 [1940], 263 [§XVIII].

the concept of time proposed by German Enlightenment philosopher Immanuel Kant and his 20th century student, Martin Heidegger.

The becoming of no-time

When IBM built a machine that finally defeated the reigning world chess champion, Garry Kasparov, in the late 1990s, it heralded the end of a time in which had been possible to believe that humans were smarter than computers in a certain sense: the kind of means-ends rationality we associate with chess turned out to be a game more suited to machines than to humans. As Kasparov noted, the eponymous Big Blue computer won out on "sheer number crunching".[25] The ability to compute the outcome of a decidedly greater number of moves than its human opponent made it the new champion. In consequence, the kind of chess power inaugurated by Big Blue is now available to anyone on their personal computer: it is no longer possible to claim that humans' ability to employ the kind of utilitarian logic necessary to win a game of chess is greater than the ability of computers. It would seem as if computers have outsmarted us.

There is another index of the superior claims to mastery made by computers in the workings of the so-called rational animal, or the agent circumscribed by the rules of bounded rationality. After it was demonstrated that those actors who conform to the largest extent to the predictions given by the rational actor-model were children at the age of five, the social theorist Jon Elster had further evidence to support his claim that the agent of rational choice theory is "implausible".[26] The agent posited by *homo oeconomicus* is more machine-like than human, and the ability to master and govern this kind of agent would lie more in the domain of computers than human beings.

To a philosopher like Martin Heidegger, these findings would come as no surprise. By circumscribing rationality as the most efficient way of achieving a goal, the domain of rationality is limited to such an extent that what we gen-

---

[25] Kasparov 2010.
[26] Behavioural economics has shown that those who tend to conform to the largest degree to the predictions of rational choice theory are children of age of 3-4. Jon Elster points at two limitations to rational choice theory: "on the one hand, people behave irrationally and this to a surprising degree considering that we were able to land a man on the moon (which is undeniably an achievement of rationality), and, on the other hand, the theory of rational choice is very unspecific insofar as it does not just prescribe what the agents must say (or do). And it is precisely in this context that I refer to science fiction, since some practitioners of rational choice theory appear to assume that agents have an almost infinite capacity for instant complex calculations" (Guénard, Florent, and Landemore, Hélène 2008, 2).

erally refer to as that kind of wisdom which affirms rest, contentment and questioning would be excluded.

There are at least three ways to counter the kind of logic that undergirds means-ends rationality as the *only* or *superior* form of knowledge. First, is human knowledge is limited to the agent posited by rational choice theory, we are confronted with an agent that is machine-like to the extent that it provides us with an unrealistic portrait of human actors.[27] Second, it is possible to distinguish between knowledge and truth and assign the former to the level of psychoanalytic drives, while the latter is associated with wisdom and desire. This strategy is employed by Slavoj Žižek when he shows that there is a *drive* for knowledge that tends to realise its own extinction: there is always more to be known, but what is lost in this inexhaustible thirst for information is the sense of lack as constitutive of desire. It is when we are able to step out of the insane pursuit of yet more data that we are able to reflect on what we truly desire. In fact, a variant of this kind of insight is incorporated into later versions of rational choice theory. Here, the agent will arrive at a point when he recognises the futility of detecting and computing yet more alternatives and that any further search for options would simply serve only to postpone the inevitable act.

The third way to question the basis of the notion that means-ends rationality should be considered our primary form of knowledge is to introduce philosophical and metaphysical consciousness. To Martin Heidegger, the sense of utilitarian rationality undermines itself when it is confronted with wonder and questioning. Following Hegel, Heidegger found that pure Being and pure Nothing belong together:

> Human existence can relate to beings only if it holds itself out into the nothing. Going beyond beings occurs in the essence of Dasein. But this *going beyond* is metaphysics itself. This implies that metaphysics belongs to the "nature of man". ...Metaphysics is the basic occurrence of Dasein. It is Dasein itself. Because the truth of metaphysics dwells in this groundless ground it stands in closest proximity to the constantly lurking possibility of deepest error. For this reason no account of scien-

---

[27] "Sometimes it is impossible to estimate the marginal cost and benefits of information. Consider a general in the midst of battle who does not know the exact disposition of the enemy troops. The value of more information, while potentially great, cannot be ascertained. Determining the expected value would require a highly implausible ability to form numerical estimates concerning the possible enemy positions" (Elster 1989, 15-16).

tific rigour attains to the seriousness of metaphysics. Philosophy can never be measured by the standard of the idea of science.[28]

To Heidegger, *Dasein* – the *being there* (Da-sein) of a being – is the essential, transcendental truth of a being that transposes it from a finite and determinate object into an immediate and indeterminate thing. This transposition amounts to hold Being out into the nothing, and it is only in so far as it is suspended in this indeterminate space that it can relate to us *as essence*. Such is also the case with human existence itself. When we position it as an indeterminate presence, it longer takes the finite, determinate individual as its object, but, rather, the Absolute of human-ness in its confrontation with the Nothing.

This movement – from concrete, finite and mediate to universal, essential and immediate – is what Heidegger referred to as the *transcending* operation, and this elemental transposition is constitutive of his notion of the metaphysical. By *moving beyond* the finite and singular, we can begin to specify the essential qualities of Being and arrive at "the ground of wonder – the revelation of nothing".

It is as a form of wonder and questioning that Heidegger announced the advent of a possible time-less time – a clearing where the light of Being could shine through and reveal to us things as they *really are*. This situation of *essential indeterminacy* is no small matter: already Kant was well aware of the sense in which each and every object arrives to us prepackaged, as it were, in categories of time, space and causality. An object is an object to us in so far as it is located in space, it is ordered in a temporal sequence, and it has some kind of causal relation to other objects.[29] However, Kant also noted that behind these *apriori* moulds that enable our thought and perception of an object there is a more essential and more elementary object, what Kant referred to as the Thing-itself (*das Ding-as-sich*). This Thing has objective existence, and it is our prerogative to ponder it, but it is nevertheless constantly slipping beyond our perceptual grasp. If there is a potential region in which we *can* grasp this Thing, it would be in Heidegger's clearing, where the light of Enlightenment would reveal to us its proper ground.

Our existence – or, in Heidegger's inventive typography, our ex-istence – lies, as it were, outside ourselves: we are most ourselves when we are posited

---

[28] Heidegger, What is metaphysics? 2008, 57, emphasis added.
[29] "The possibility of sensuous objects is a relation of these objects to thought, in which something (the empirical form) may be cogitated a priori; while that which constitutes the matter — the reality of the phenomenon (that element which corresponds to sensation) — must be given from without, as otherwise it could not even be cogitated by, nor could its possibility be presentable to the mind" (Kant 1899, 326).

ecstatically to our being, i.e., in a relation that takes as its operative criteria a *moving beyond* itself and a placing of our being within the domain of the Nothing.[30] To Heidegger,

> man occurs essentially in such a way that he is the "there" [das "*Da*"], that is, the clearing of Being. The "Being" of the *Da*, and only it, has the fundamental character of ex-istence, that is, of an ecstatic inherence in the truth of Being.[31]

Man is what gives the *there* to the being-there, an intranscendtable moment of the presence of the Being. Heidegger would reintroduce Kant's comments on time's essential unfolding on the subject to show how we are constantly becoming subject of and against time: "as pure self-affection [*reine Selbaffektion*], time is not an effective affect that encounters an already existing self, but in so far as it is pure it moulds the very essence of affecting oneself [*sich-selbst-Angehen*]".[32]

Our scientific view of the rock that we inhabit holds that our planet has been around for 4-5 billion years, shaped from the gathering together of matter, turned into oceans and land by volcanic activity and made habitable after having cooled down and with the emission of free oxygen into the atmosphere about a billion years later. This story contains all the four elements in the quadrants of Empedocles and Heidegger: land and ocean, air and fire. The element of fire, which, in Heidegger's variant, becomes the domain of the Gods, relates to the Earth as the Sun to the planets: it provided the matter necessary to form the plants and animals, the heat required to keep us warm, and the light necessary for our sight. Above all, the Sun was what the planets were made from – it was there prior to the planets – and it will exist after the planets have exited the world stage. It is in *this* sense that Sun as the ball of fire appears to stretch far beyond the limited possibilities of our planet. It is as if Empedocles' element of fire stands to air as the immortality of the Gods stands to the mortals of Heidegger's diagram.

Another way of considering the distinction, not between land and ocean, sky and earth, but between fire and air, Gods and mortals, is to think in terms of Hegel's notion of the Absolute. To him, only a human existence that allows for a record could conceivably participate in – i.e., be self-consciously a part of – the Absolute. This is why nomadic existence would be forever left out of the universal history of mankind: their inability to write down laws that per-

---

[30] Lacan illustrates this relation with the donut-shaped *torus*, see figure 1.1 above.
[31] Heidegger, Letter on Humanism 2008, 156.
[32] Heidegger, Kant und das Problem der Metaphysik 1991, 189.

sist across generations, their lack of tools to record their histories and common experiences, and their deprivation of techniques to learn from previous experience in a complex and intergenerational way would disallow their participation in Universal history.

While it would seem as if the nomad provides Guy Debord with a kind of heroic figure that stands *against* the cumulative technological know-how that has produced specialisation, mass production, commodity fetishism, and those trappings of modernity that we now have a more tempered view on, it is also clear that such a figure could only persist on so far as it would become adaptive to the very technological environment it would be enlisted to overcome.

Nevertheless, Debord subscribed to Hegel's view that it was only with the advent of relatively stable communities enabled by farming and the agricultural mode of life that it was possible to produce a record of laws and history, and to maintain scripts that were held to be sacred and that provided instructions for the invocation and praising of Absolute Being. It is logical that the notion of time we have inherited through the mediating religious institutions hold repetitive temporal structures and cyclical recurrences to capture the essence of time.

The scientific view of planetary time – from its inception some 4-5 billion years ago, through a series of cosmic and geological events to the earth we have made our home today – as a linear and homogeneous unfolding only became prominent and, later, seen as the *natural* way of perceiving time with the onset of printing presses that enabled a relatively rapid diffusion of narratives written in local scripts, journals promoting a time-scale that propagated a sense of *simultaneity across time*, and, finally, a social unfolding that detached what had been colonial dependencies from their previous imperial masters. These new entities – nations – had relatively autonomous time-scales – an event could take place in Lime while *something else* happened in Madrid or Rio – that facilitated a new kind of historicism: a view of the world where events were recorded according to their placement on a universal, linear and homogeneous time-scale.

This view on time is what we are living under today. However, as already Kant pointed out, it is not the *only* way to consider the incursion of time in our existence. It is not that, Kant would say, an already formed self would encounter a time that is moving along seamlessly, but our sense of time contributes to the way we shape ourselves. In essence, Kant would claim, time is merely a category of thought and perception. It has no ground in the object *itself* – an object of which we can know very little, and yet of which it is our prerogative to think and contemplate. This *thing-in-itself* [*das Ding-an-sich*] is what stands out into the Nothing – to borrow Heidegger's phrase – as the being that gives us the light and that is being illuminated through our unceasing questioning, wonder and praise.

It is what gives us our ground – or, as Heidegger would put it, our groundless ground – to keep on questioning our existence.[33]

---

[33] The "groundless ground" of questioning in Heidegger refers to his extension of "the old proposition ex nihilo nihil fit [to] ex nihilo omne ens qua ens fit:" from the nothing all beings as beings come to be (Heidegger, What is metaphysics? 2008, 56, 57).

Chapter 3

Knowing the rock

In the opening pages of Karl Ove Knausgård's *My Struggle* (2007-2011) the narrator ponders the difference between a world that is *known* and a world that is *meaningful*.[1] We generally tend to hold the view that knowledge dispels superstition and the darkness that envelops us. This perspective has become so ingrained in us that there is an idiomatic expression that holds that "everything can be explained by using our sense of logic", i.e., by applying the tenets of rationality. However, the narrator of *My Struggle* takes the almost diametrically opposite view, namely that a world that is known stands in precise *opposition* to the sense of this saying. Rather, he contends, the *more* we know the world, the less *meaningful* it is.

We should understand a world that is meaningful as a statement on the nature of *truth*: to know is something else and different from having arrived at truth, or, even, to be truth*ful*. It is as if we use knowledge, in the sense of *facts* and *realities*, to *hide* and *disguise* truth. It arrives to us as a strategy of avoidance: as Sigmund Freud would say, truth is what we are left with when we have discarded all our rationalisations and habits of escape.

In short, what Knausgård's narrator realises is that by rendering the world mysterious and unknown, we are in effect making the world meaningful. Is this not a stance that is indistinguishable from a full-blown embrace of irrationalism and darkness? No, it is, rather, a view that is fully compatible with the existentialist tradition, and which is made particularly vivid in the post-Auschwitz writing of the psychoanalyst Victor Frankl, a one-time student of Freud's.

What was it that made the prisoner of the death camp survive? This question is the key preoccupation of Frankl's most well-known exposition of camp life.[2] The answer he arrives at is not a simple calculation of the number of corpses an inmate would have seen on an average day, the number of blows received by the wardens, the amount of degradation and sheer filth that the prisoner would have to endure, but, in fact, the exact opposite: it is *after* all these *knowledges* have been arrived at and dispelled as inconsequential and

---

[1] *Min kamp*, whose title, in Germanic languages, resonates vividly with the autobiography of another and historically more notorious author in the tradition of *Einfühlung*, *Adolf Hitler* (Knausgård 2007-2011).
[2] Frankl 1992.

meaningless that the inmate can arrive at the only truly important question that will enable him to survive – should I live or die?

This question is the existential moment, and to Frankl it is beyond doubt that it is a question that is absolutely essential for the survival of human beings at their utmost deprivation. In our darkest hour, Frankl contends, we are still left with a choice, and it is this choice that renders us human. It is our encounter with existence itself.

What we have is a moment of *not-knowing*. What is crucial is not the amount of so-called sense-data or accumulated proof we can muster, but our sheer confrontation with the beyond. It is our struggle with the Nothing. To be *truthful* is something else and other than to *know*, or, to put it differently, to have *knowledge* is in a certain sense not the same as knowing the *truth*.

For these reasons we should still remain puzzled in front of the ancient *scholiasts* of philosophy in Athens, and the inscription on the entrance to the temple of Apollo at Delphi: "gnōthi seauton", *know thyself*. Is it not so, we should ponder, that what was *most* central to the ancients was *not* the nature of *Phusis* – the physical, material world – but something that is essentially beyond measure and that has no material substance – ourselves, our soul?

Approaching truth as something that is not in its essence simple and clear-cut, but, rather, complex and ambiguous is noted as something that gives great force already by Plato.[3] Nevertheless, the connection between the *force* of idiomatic expressions and their *meaning* is opaque and cumbersome. Plato seems to suggest that their force derives precisely from their ambiguity and that they demand an effort on the side of the listener to make sense.

In other words, in these cases meaning is not immanent to language *itself*. Truth appears to us through what we experience as an *unveiling*, and, by the same token, a *veiling*, as if, on walking in a forest, light falls on certain objects, illuminating them and making them appear to us, only to, in the next instant, become obstructed by some leaf or tree, and, in effect, letting the same object withdraw into obscurity. It is in *this* sense we speak of *insight* as a form of knowledge: vision indicates something beyond mere perception and the rec-

---

[3] Socrates enlists "Thales of Miletus, Pittacus of Mytilene, Bias of Priene, Solon of our city, Cleobulus of Lindus, Myson of Chen, and, last of the traditional seven, Chilon of Sparta [as] enthusiasts, lovers and disciples of the Spartan culture; and you can recognise that character in their wisdom by the short, memorable sayings that fell from each of them they assembled together. ... Their philosophy had this style of laconic brevity" (Plato, Protagoras 1967, 343a-b).

ord of the eye, and this surplus takes the metaphorical form of a vision of the *interior* – a sight inwards, or an *in*-sight.[4]

Truth and psychoanalysis

Freud made a more distinct emphasis on the sense we have of being at the receiving end of an *experience*. His term for what is indicative of such an encounter is aha-*Erlebnis*, highlighting how the subject achieves the insight only in the presence of an *Other*, an instance that holds the power to provide the Law.[5] It is as if we say to ourselves, "so *that's* how it was", and that this knowledge was only revealed to *us* at the moment of visionary insight – aha-*Erlebnis* – while it was known and acknowledged by the Other all along.

What we have here is a distinction between the truth *in* and the truth *of* psychoanalysis: while we can say that through analytic work, the subject arrives at some kind of insight into himself, psychoanalysis itself makes more general and universal claims to truth. The former – the analysand's working-through of his subjective situation – is what we refer to as the *talking cure*, which is, by its very nature, subjective and contingent upon experiences and insights made by the analysand himself.

The latter has been a subject of some debate. There has been made claims to the effect that psychoanalysis, and in particular analysis in the tradition of Freud and Lacan, *has no* core, which is to say that there *is no* truth to psychoanalysis itself. Analysts such as Slavoj Žižek takes a clear stand *against* such readings of Freud and Lacan. Rather than a practice without a core, Žižek finds that psychoanalysis is a way of understanding the world that has not one, but *three* core assumptions. These are universals: the hidden revelation of what we usually refer to as the Oedipus complex, the fear experienced by the son in the encounter with the father (so-called *fear of castration*), and the necessary element of *transference* in the psychoanalytic encounter.[6]

There is an element of truth in psychoanalysis that transverses the subjective and becomes *objective* truth: it is the truth of psychoanalysis itself. In order to understand the boundaries that constitute psychoanalytic *practice* – i.e., the work of analysis that involves an analysand's engagement with himself – it is necessary to understand that these limits are constituted by psychoanalysis *itself*. Lacan was very clear on the notion of *prophetic speech*: this

---

[4] Paul de Man's *Blindness and Insight* (1989) provides the authoritative exposition of sight as metaphor for knowledge in the Romantic tradition.
[5] Lacan borrows this term from Wolfgang Köhler's research on primates (Lacan, Aggressiveness in psychoanalysis 2006, 75).
[6] Žižek, Is it possible to traverse the fantasy in cyberspace? 1999, 123.

is not the ramblings of a madman, some crisis-struck self-mutilator, or some sacrosanct divination. Rather, the kind of speech we recognise as prophetic *as such* properly demarcates the *beginning* of the psychoanalytic encounter.[7] On the other end of the stretch that we refer to as the analytic labour stands a subject that *fully shoulders the responsibility of the Law*, i.e., who is able to completely comprehend and affirm the position of the Father. Between these two moments – the prophet announcing himself and the assumption of the rôle of the father – is a searching practice of what Anna O., one of Freud's early patients, called *chimney sweeping*: it is a close encounter with oneself that enables the subject to arrive at a truth that is surely subjective, but which is held out into the objective through the analytic encounter.

It is at the boundaries of analysis that the *analyst* and the *analysand* go different ways. The analyst, endowed with the proper measures of treatment, arrives at the encounter with a cargo of analytic experience, and, when the treatment has come to an end, the analyst is set to continue his work with *other* analysands. The client is limited in his engagement with psychoanalytic practice to this singular encounter. What this should tell us is that there is a difference in knowledge and power that is *played out* in the analytic relationship. The term Freud used to describe the mechanism of analysis that relates to this distinction between analyst and analysand was *transference*.

In Lacan's approach to Freud, transference receives the name of *subject-supposed-to-know*. It is from the very beginning as if the analyst *knows something* about the analysand's desire that is not, or at least *not yet*, explicated. The work required on the part of the analysand to make the encounter a psychoanalytic moment is to affirm the analyst as positioned in the rôle of the one who *knows something* about the subject of analysis. This mysterious *something* becomes the very kernel of analysis: what is this *it* that the analysand believes the analyst to know, and how would it be possible to incorporate such knowledge into the subjective world of the analysand?

The position in which the analysand locates the analyst closely resembles the space that Lacan allotted to the instance of the Other in *Schema L*.[8] This instance is the place from which the Law is instantiated and articulated. In a

---

[7] Notice that Lacan's encounter with "prophetic" speakers in the 1930s led him to theorise the relation between psychosis and Biblical prophecy: they both engage an ambiguous kind of "mid speak", that makes it possible to speak the truth while avoiding the whole truth (Kunze 1988).

[8] Lacan gives two versions of *Schema L*, the first in his essay on "The purloined letter" (2006, 40), and a second, simplified version in his seminar on psychosis (On a question prior to any possible treatment of psychosis 2006, 458). Note that the terms on the imaginary axis (*a* and *a'*) are reversed in the simplified version. See also figure 5.1.

very strict sense, it is in the Other that the subject comes into being. The question the subject would have with regard to existence in being is therefore primarily directed to this Other, and by inserting the analyst into this position, it is with the view of a reformulation of the connections between the subject and the Other through analysis.

Since the intervention of the Other in the imaginary relation between the child and his primary caretaker is closely related to the phallic function – what Lacan would designate as the Symbolic Order – it is of particular interest to consider cases where the instance of the Other is maintained by someone other than the father.[9] One example Lacan studied with the view of demonstrating the non-necessary relation between the father and the phallic function was Shakespeare's *Hamlet*.[10] In this play, the protagonist is deprived of his father *before* the play starts (which contrasts with the fable of Oedipus, where the protagonist removes his father in the course of the play), and this sets into motion a series of interludes and soliloquies in which the son turns to ponder the meaning of his father's absence and the sense of his relation to the Law.

What Lacan showed in his study was that it is Hamlet's *mother* – Gertrude – that maintains the phallic function in the play. In the absence of Hamlet's biological father, her son turns to her as the beholder of the Father's name, with the effect that Hamlet is positioned in a double bind: should he take up the quest assigned to him by his father's ghost so as to seek revenge against Claudius – who has taken up the position of Hamlet's step-father – or should he heed the word of his mother and resign to the repeated experience of his uncle having his way with his mother? Lacan will ask us to consider how Hamlet's indecision is contingent upon his mother's indecision, and how this contingency shows the extent to which the subject's desire depends on the desire of the Other:

> Hamlet does not choose. His mother does not choose because of something present inside her, like an instinctive voracity. The sacrosanct genital object that we recently added to our technical vocabulary appears to her as an object to be enjoyed [*objet d'une jouissance*] in what is truly the direct satisfaction of a need, and nothing else. This is the aspect that makes Hamlet waver in his abjuration of his mother.[11]

It is when the mother in the next instance throws herself into the arms of the, to Hamlet, degraded and despicable uncle Claudius, that Hamlet must again confront his inability to make his mother abstain from further intercourse. Her fall,

---

[9] Lacan, Seminar on 'The purloined letter' 2006, 10.
[10] Lacan, Desire and the interpretation of desire in Hamlet 1982.
[11] Ibid., 12-13.

what Lacan referred to as her "abandon", shows the zeal which Hamlet always in is always in deficit. As Lacan noted, "the dependence of [Hamlet's] desire on the Other subject forms the permanent dimension of [his] drama".[12] Here we have a case where the "Thou art that!" – given flesh through Gertrude as the instantiation of Hamlet's Ideal Ego – serves as the inner kernel of subjective truth, so that, in the case of Hamlet, the notion of a subject that is articulated as an *aspect of* the Other, while also coming into being as an act of *separation from* the mother/Other, leaves Hamlet dishevelled and unable to act. The solution he will find is to take up the cause as his lost father's champion in a duel against Claudius' stand-in. The dilemma of the double function of Hamlet's mother *is* thus resolved, even if the resolution will come at a time when it is only Fortinbras who remains to assemble the shards of the Danish kingdom.

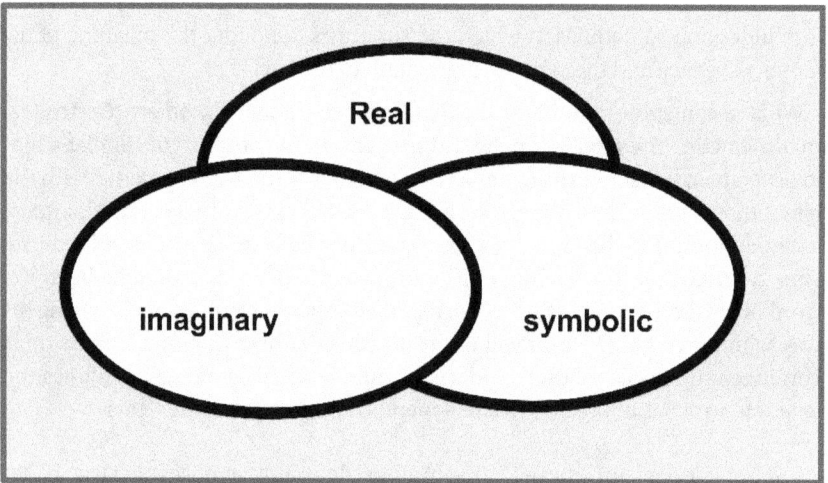

Figure 3.1: Triad - Venn diagram of Lacan's triadic typology.

What is required to clarify Gertrude's relation to Hamlet is to introduce the triadic domains of Real – Imaginary – Symbolic (see figure 3.1). In terms of the coming-into-being of the subject, which, in this context is primarily centred around Hamlet, what is our first concern is the relation between the Imaginary and the Symbolic. In so far as the relation between the infant and the mother is an imaginary relation, their liaison can only be severed through the intervention of the phallic function, i.e., the father, through which the child is

---

[12] Ibid., 13.

introduced to the Symbolic.[13] What is clear is that with the inauguration of the child into the Symbolic Order, it is an entailment that the subject that is formed is also a subject *of desire*, i.e., the child that was entirely shaped as an aspect of the psychoanalytic drives now becomes a subject of articulation. It can express its wishes – or refrain from expressing them – in a symbolic system that is organised through certain lacunae and regulations. There are forbidden objects, and one such object is precisely the child's primary caretaker. Since she is also the father's object of desire, she receives the emblem of illegality in the newly formed desiring subject's psycho-sexual universe.

Subsequently, the reason why there is a *gap* in Gertrude's accomplishments vis-a-vis the Symbolic Order and the phallic function has to do with the domain of the Real – what Lacan gave the expression "the Real of sexual reproduction".[14] What we should take note of is that there is no *direct* relation between what takes the form as a *barring* of the mother as Other – a result of her double configuration as mother and the one who instantiates the Law – and the psychoanalytic process of *sexuation*. This latter concept is linked to the formation of the subject as it ushers into the symbolic domain. Gertrude's barring is entirely linked to the Real, which is to say that what Hamlet experiences in relation to the Other with regards to his stalling and indecision is an effect of the *foreclosure of the Real*.

There is an insurmountable boundary here, and when Gertrude cannot – however much she would have wanted to – fully enter into the rôle that was occupied by Hamlet's father it has to do precisely with this foreclosure. Moreover, this is why Hamlet provides an even more succinct expression of the phallic function as *structural event*. The father is gone – as was the case for Oedipus earlier – and the only way for Hamlet to continue his communication with the father *as distinct signifier* is to address him as a ghost on the roof of the castle Elsinore, since it would provide for our protagonist the required grounding to be able to claim retribution from Gertrude's new lover and husband. Nevertheless, the Law Hamlet ultimately answers to – and this is something he is perfectly aware of – does not usher from his biological father, or, rather, it does not *any longer* usher from his father, and this is precisely what sustains him towards his actions. Only the Law as it is issued through the phallic function as symbolic event would suffice to provide for Hamlet the reason he needs to complete the mission he believes that he has, and this Law can only be partially expressed by Gertrude.

---

[13] See also the discussion on the formation of the subject through the three phases of the mirror stage on page 30.
[14] Žižek, Holding the place 2000, 327. See also the discussion of the Real on page 21.

To Lacan truth and desire were intimately linked. In so far as we can associate knowledge with the drives – in the sense that it is reasonable to say that there is a *drive for knowledge* – truth pertains to the symbolic order and the assumption of the phallic function. If there is any truth to psychoanalysis *as such*, this is precisely what we're in for: a codification of an experience of truth, and this truth is not strictly subjective. When Lacan, as Heidegger before him, spoke of the ex-centric subject, it was with reference to the way that we are most intimate to this kernel of truth at the moment when we stand outside ourselves, what Heidegger referred to as the ex-static subject. It is in *this* sense that we can speak of *being in truth*: it is a state of existence, a state of exaltation and a reciprocal relation of giving and praising through which the subject receives his most distinct token.

The advent and the gift

In so far as truth exists as a state of being, the relation between the subject's being and existence indicates the sense in which we are *within the true*. It is an experience of arriving at a clearing where truth is *unconcealed* – however momentarily – as if by revelation. This sense of arrival is what Heidegger would describe as the *advent*: it is something that awaits us as much as something we await. In other words, the kernel of truth arrives as a *gift* that can only be received by a subject who makes no demand. It is when we least expect it that we are granted access to the clearing.

There is a sense in which this notion of truth stands in *direct opposition* to the kind of truth enunciated by logical positivism: in so far as some object relation can be *expressed* in a language that can be verified as having an empirical correlate, it is *not* the essence of truth that Heidegger set out to delineate. What we have instead is a truth that is sensible, but that continues to evade our symbolic apparatus, so that it has as its essence a site that lies *beyond* the domain of linguistic utterability. This notion of truth requires an approach that has a mode of address that differs from the positivist language. It is as if we seek ways in which the clearing can be addressed while accounting for the sense in which it can never be fully apparent.

This question of bringing truth into being while acknowledging the sense it continues to evade our abilities to grasp it lies at the heart of Jacques Derrida's notion of the presence: it is a term he derives from Heidegger. For instance, in the latter's work on the truth in art, Heidegger foregrounds how it is the work of the critic, and, as an unavoidable consequence, the artwork itself, to bring truth into presence.[15] This *presencing* of truth indicates a way in

---

[15] Heidegger, The origin of the work of art 2008.

which art and art criticism enable us to approach the clearing. It is when darkness lifts, light is thrown upon the earth, and we can see clearly so as to distinguish what *is* from what *is not* that we have a sense of a knot that is being untangled – and clearing-up [*Aufklärung*] of darkness.

The advent of this kind of light indicates the sense in which truth has been brought into our presence. It is as if we, in our ordinary lives, go about with a relation to truth that is *approximate*, but nevertheless fully sufficient. What Derrida tried to grasp with his notion of the trace is the sense in which truth, while never fully present, is still in our surroundings, so that it is possible to find its trace. This trace can be tracked so as to bring us closer to the kernel of truth, and it is *this* process that Derrida referred to as the work of *deconstruction*.

Deconstruction relies on an unacknowledged *gap* between two concepts that are brought into a dualist relationship, e.g., mind and body, culture and nature, or writing and speech. It is our habitual way of the world, Derrida would have it, that we hold the latter of these notions in the higher esteem than the former, so that the body appears to have precedence over mind, nature has primacy over culture, and speech is close to thought than writing. What Derrida sought to show was that this ontological relation of domination was arbitrary and could be overturned, so that the former concept would have primacy, or that, simply, the relation of dominance would be rendered obsolete.

For instance, when we approach language, we tend to assume that speech has the more intimate relation to thought. This relation comes out both when we discuss cultural artefacts of a historical nature, so that the rhapsodists of the Homeric age are held to be closer to the kernel of truth of the Odyssey than the textual variants that have been handed down to us, but also in our contemporary stance to what is considered to be our most intimate and sincere expressions of our opinions, so that when polls and surveys are conducted, oral interviews, focus groups, and other forms of *spontaneous verbal expressions* seem to have a high degree of truth value. In relation to this elevation of orality as a medium of truth, the written word would appear to only be able to convey a derived and secondary articulation. However, what Derrida sought to show was how writing compels us to clarify a more complex and subtle relationship to truth, and thus dispel some of the more mundane and idiomatic utterances that we often resort to in spontaneous verbal interaction.

To Derrida, it is in the gap between speech and writing that it is possible to discern the trace of Being. Consider for a moment the perceptions we have of the relation between speech and writing, or, more precisely, the origin of the written code. Jorge Luis Borges reminded us that to the medieval Nordic mind, those who had knowledge of the written word were perceived as being in possession of some mysterious, mystical power. For how could it be that some sign on wood or inscription in a rock could *stand for* sounds, words and so be made meaningful? Surely, the analphabet would think, such a skill could only be connected to some supernatural power, and to engage in writing would amount to nothing less than to practice magic.[16]

Now, even this, apparently unknowledgeable and spurious approach to writing has some substance to it. For instance, when Ferdinand de Saussure approached the sign, he would conceive of it as a *sound-image*, i.e., while the verbal utterance – the phonemic imprint, as it were – had primacy, he retained the notion of the sign's visual potentiality, the image. Already here the relation between the two – the auditory and the visual imprints – are unclear and charged with complexity. Should we regard the written code as derived and secondary to the spoken word? If writing is simply a transliteration of speech, how are we to approach the sense in which distinctions in written languages today often have no correlatives in speech, and, even more to the point, how should we consider the notion of so-called *non-natural* languages, such as computer code?

What we are confronted with in these considerations is a distinct and unassimilable *gap* between speech and writing, and, while each form of communication is in some ways translatable to the other, the relation between the two is opaque and complex. In other words, the transition from speech to writing, and vice versa releases us into a state of *indeterminacy*. When we can no longer determine which element is primary to the other, whether it is *speech* that *signifies* writing, or the other way around, and the extent to which we can say that speech or writing is closer and more intimate with our thoughts, we are released into a state of wonderment and questioning. We simply cannot decide which of the two elements is prior to the other, and it is this notion of *undecidability* that to Derrida is the very passage into philosophy.

Deconstruction can be considered as a way to *move us* into wonderment and *release us* from preconceived certainties that, on close inspection, turn out to be grounded in unstable and shifting notions. In other words, what is achieved through deconstructive inspection is a shedding of prejudices so as to bring us closer to truth, even when this sense of truth is *different from* the kinds of certainties that we associate with the sciences. It is here that we find the distinctive character of philosophy as a form of engagement with the world: while the scientific mind seeks uncancellable knowledges, philosophy relishes in precisely that which is *not* finally determinate.

It is here that we can begin to understand the distinction between knowledge and truth. While it is possible to consider a catalogue of scientific truth, which, nevertheless would have to be subject to a continuing upgrading

---

[16] See Borges 2002, 96-98, Skeat 1888, 510.

Knowing the rock 53

and revision and science revised its database, such a catalogue would be inconceivable in the realm of truth. It is through the engagement with questions and indeterminacy that truth *reveals itself* to us, and it is this revelatory character, or, as Heidegger would put it, unconcealment, that the clearing announces its advent. Subsequently, being in the nearness of truth cannot be reduced to an enumerative relation.[17]

To understand Derrida's approach to deconstruction, it is crucial to appreciate how he – in a way that is strictly analogous to Heidegger – engaged in a critique of Plato that nevertheless sought to re-establish the latter as a foundational figure of philosophy. In "Plato's pharmacy", Derrida noted how Plato in *Phaedrus* condemns writing, while praising speech, precisely on the grounds that the spoken word has a more intimate relation to truth in Plato. The complexity in Derrida's engagement with Plato's derision of writing comes out at it most distinct in the way that he would put to use the sense in which Phaedrus leaves us with an indeterminate relation to spoken and written communication: in the same way as writing is a *pharmakon*, i.e., a cure, against forgetting and despotism, and so a means to further wisdom and power, it is also a poison, since it deprives the one who governs from immediately asserting his spoken will into acts of governance.

In *Phaedrus*, Plato recounts the mythical origin of writing. At the time when Thamus was ruler of Egypt, the inventor Teuth presented the king with a whole range of new technologies: numbers, calculation, geometry and astronomy, dices and board games, but first and foremost writing [*grammata*].[18] While the technology of writing is presented by Teuth as a gift, Derrida noted how such a donation would only receive its meaning on its recognition as such by its recipient. In other words, only by acknowledging the gift *as a present* would it be made meaningful as an object of exchange. However, in Plato's recollection if the myth, the king refuses to receive the gift. What seemed to be a technique of power that would extend the ruler's domain – and, as a consequence endow its inventor with the prestige associated with having invented and donated such a technology – is instead reduced to a skill without value, recognition or even existence.

The reason for the discrepancy between Teuth's expectations and Thamus' act of rejection should be sought in the distance between the king-God's way of governing – this is a ruler that asserts his domain though speech and dictation, and whose spoken word is sufficient to effectuate an

---

[17] "*In-die-Nähe*", translated as "moving-into-nearness" (Heidegger, Discourse on Thinking 1966, 86-89).
[18] Plato, Phaedrus 1892, 484, Derrida, Plato's pharmacy 1981. See also Johnson 1981, xxiv-xxvi.

act – and the question of a supplement to his orders: would not a written record simply *limit* the potentiality of governance in a culture of analphabetism? Thamus responds by not only unacknowledging writing *as a gift*, but also by admonishing it as an aberration. Writing should be regarded as a misdeed and immediately abandoned.

Derrida would note how Thamus acts as a father in relation to a novel idea from one of his sons, and *as* a father he remains suspicious. How will such a technology alter the relations of power in the house of Thamus? The position of the Father, Derrida noted, was as the *origin* of words, and as a father he who speaks supports his words with his power. However, words that have been spoken would fall apart without the presence of their father: utterances need an origin to speak in their behalf, to answer interjections, and to give them grounds. Without the father's presence, words would be reduced to nothing but writing. This perspective is intimately linked to the position of the father: the specificity of writing in Plato is inextricably entwined with the absence of the Father.

It follows that the *cure* or writing also has a dark underside: is not the urge to write embedded with the wish to get rid of the father, so that the technology of writing is a *poisoned present*, i.e., *pharmakon* not in the sense of *cure*, but as *poison*? Written words are orphans. They have no father present to defend them, neither in the legal nor moral sense. Speech, on the other hand, is alive with a living father who is present, standing behind or by his word, maintaining and caring for it in his own house. Speech is a living being that adapts to circumstance and to the expectations and demands of those who participate in a discussion and who listens. While writing is a dead body, Derrida noted, speech is a living existence.

The supplementary character of the written word in relation to speech in Plato heralds a view of signification in which the question of *absence* comes to the fore. Plato's demonstration of the speaker not being present in the case of written discourse becomes a hallmark of *all* signification in the psychoanalysis of Jacques Lacan: here, desire – which can *only* be pronounced in speech – is forever entangled in the logic of lack, since we can only want that which we do not already have. Speech can be perceived as an attempt to bring an other – some object of desire – into being, and it is in *this* sense that we can regard discourse as *doubly haunted* in Lacan. Not only is writing marked by its author's absence, but *all* communication is similarly characterised by the absence of a desired object.[19]

Analogous to the enhanced presence of truth in spoken discourse vis-a-vis written texts is Plato's view on truth telling in public speech compared to the kinds of utterances we find in the arts. When Plato in *The Republic* is quite clear that drama and poetry can have no positive purpose in the Athenian democracy, it is because the notion of truthfulness in these genres – their *ways* of telling their truths – are secondary and derived when compared to philosophical and political utterances in the public space. In other words, speech stands for writing as philosophy or politics stand for the arts.

What is the kind of *stance* provided by the supplement in relation to the primary form of communication? This question is crucial and provides the key to understand the prominence of spoken words and dialogue as the preeminent genres of truth telling in Plato. Writing appears as first and foremost a technique to *write down* or *transcribe* words that have already been given expression in speech. They have no autonomous domain in their own right, and their continued existence beyond the actual presence of the speaker or writer makes them a potentially dangerous tool that can be turned against he who spoke or wrote the text since it can form a ground against which later utterances can be measured or compared. Truth is clearly not something that can be catalogued and archived in Plato: the shifting and dialogic elements of truth telling is foregrounded time and again when Socrates comes up against interlocutors who believe they have established absolute knowledge once and for all.[20]

When Derrida would speak of the trace as a component of signification and meaning, he was indicating a relation that nevertheless went beyond the non-presence of the speaker in our reading. Rather, he sought to show how there remains a sense in which the meaning cannot be fully captured, even when we resort to terms such as intentionality and denotation/connotation. The source of the absence, not of the author as meaning granting instance, but of any absolute position that could make utterances meaningful in any exhaustive sense lies in the fact that we cannot in language determine any point of

---

[19] The absence of the author, pointed out already by Plato and brought into relief by Derrida, should be grounded in a *differently* inflected desire, namely desire on the part of the reader/listener, to bring into actuality the presence of the author. In so far as the speaker is not actually available to answer questions, respond to critique, back up his words, etc., such a presence can only be assumed and taken as a postulate in deliberations over the text.
[20] See, e.g., *Cratylus* (1892) or *Phaedrus* (1892).

origin for signification. [21] This is why such an instance can only appear to us as a ghostly apparition, something that is almost or even almost not present.

Perception and forgetting

In his "Short dialogue on the indestructibility of our true being by death", Arthur Schopenhauer noted how it is that when we die our individuality – i.e., what is specific to us as distinct from the generality of the species – pass away, while what is essential to us – our universality – lives on. In a fictional dialogue, modelled on the Socratic encounters retold by Plato, Schopenhauer has Thrasymachos ask of Philalethes what will remain of him after his death. Philalethes answers that

> As an individual, with your death there will be an end of you. But your individuality is not your true and final being, indeed it is rather the mere expression of it; it is not the thing-in-itself but only the phenomenon presented in the form of time, and accordingly has both a beginning and an end. Your being in itself, on the contrary, knows neither time, nor beginning, nor end, nor the limits of a given individuality; hence no individuality can be without it, but it is there in each and all.[22]

What is crucial to understand here is that the distinction between the individual and that which is true and actual to our being is distinct and contingent entities. As long as there is a true and in-itself-existant Being there is the possibility of the individual, but the opposite does not hold true: the individual is determined by the presence of the Other, but not the other way around.

The implications of this insight are profound to the field of knowledgeability with regard to our existence. First, our individuality is limited by and contingent upon a subject that transcends and determines us. Second, this subject is not dependent on our individual existence, but continues to maintain its being beyond our limited presence. Third, this Being as a *noumenal* form of subjectivity is a distinct part of us, so that it makes sense to say that our being *continues* even *after* our individual existence has perished.

These are the reasons why Schopenhauer can claim that our individual existence serves primarily as a repository of a will that is distinct from the general force of the universal Being. It is a clam that resonates well with Hegel's notion that there is a distinction between the Absolute or Universal, on the one hand,

---

[21] An important consideration for Derrida in this regard would have been the idea that for the Jews the name of the divinity neither could nor should be uttered.
[22] Schopenhauer, Essays 1897, 93.

and the singular and particular, on the other. To participate in the Universal is contingent upon a consciousness that has a grasp that goes beyond the individual – it has a record of its history, a catalogue of laws, and an ongoing journal of singular events that serves as a common repository of belonging and Other – and such a grasp is only possible with the advent of societies that can maintain a degree of stability and prevalence in the face of forces of flux and division.

Our first lesson from Schopenhauer should be that he did affirm Kant's distinction between the world as it appears to us in the categories of time, space and causality – i.e., the world as phenomenon – and the world *in itself*, prior to and beyond such categories of thought and perception. It is this latter, *noumenal* being of the world that enabled Hegel and Schopenhauer to conceive of a Universal and Absolute that stand aside from the individual and his perceptions, and this Being had as its advent a spatial-temporal existence that went prior to and will last beyond any individual constituent entity.

Another way of considering this distinction is by way of Lacan's eccentric subject.[23] It is a notion he borrowed from Heidegger. When the latter would claim that we are most ourselves when we stand outside ourselves – i.e., when we forget our individual barricades and embarrassments – he would predate Lacan's postulate that the subject *has no interior*: there isn't any sense in which we can be most authentically ourselves by stripping away our layers of pretence and masquerade so as to arrive at our innermost and hitherto secretive essential self. We *do* have an essence, in Lacan's view of the psyche, but this core is situated on our *outside*: it is by forgetting our defence mechanisms that we can begin to act in ways that are truly in accordance with our destiny.

In the thought of Wolfgang Schirmacher, these are notions that crystallize in the form of the clone. In his philosophy of the media and mediatization, the clone is the entity by which we can conceive of ourselves in our exterior being. This is why he will note that in our contemporary hyper-reality of constantly fluctuating media projections we are in an ongoing engagement with a mediatized world of subjective cloning. For instance, the media invention Dolly the Sheep served as a figure that could hold within itself both our fears and hopes for a future where humans and other biological entities would reproduce by way of any reproductive entities, and also, and perhaps more crucially, it was an image of ourselves within a totality of media images. Thus, Dolly came to embody the very duplicate subjectivity of the exteriorised media subject – a figure that would transcend precisely the individuality of the consumer and become a vehicle to participate in a sense, or perhaps, some would claim, sense-*less* Universality.

---

[23] See also the remarks on Heidegger's notions of *Dasein* and ex-istence on page 37.

What remains of life is not so much an inner sanctum, which is to say a holy, inviolable core of existence, as much as an absence that is revealed to us as an *effect* of engagement with the subject. Since this absence can never be fully present – as much as it seems to lie at the heart of a lack that it cannot be completely satisfied or contained – it requires imaginative and symbolic work to provide it with an appearance that is perceptible. The ability to grasp the advent of the subject is not something that is equivocally and evenly distributed, and it is here that Schirmacher reserves for the artist a particular skill in rendering the clearing: it lies within the domain of the arts to render the specificity of the artistic object such that it appears in its universal being. In other words, what we have is an instance of giving appearance to the singularity of subjective existence.

In a reformulation of Nietzsche's notion of the superman, Schirmacher proposes that the gifted individual is not so much endowed with capacities that render this person better or superior in any moral or biological sense, but rather that the *Über* in *Übermensch* should stand for an enhanced ability to perceive the presencing of the artistic object when it appears as a presence. It is *this* particular skill that Schirmacher renders as *hyperperception*: an uncanny grasp on the uncovering of the essential truth of objects at the moments when they are present to be beheld.

> Hyperperception is an intensification of humankind and cannot be placed on a list of proscribed powers. More perception, of greater differentiation, finer complexity and participation is the best protection against the dressage of our gaze and emotions. Yet by the same token, forgetting is an intrinsic part of perception, our guard against the exaggeration of the historical sense, which would lead to the poisoning of memory. …A hyperperception which is equally bold in its granting and forgetting of world and which makes differentiations is effective in practice. According to the traces of a self-fulfilling life it is a hyperperception at once critical and creative.[24]

What is at stake here is the way this form of perceptive ability is juxtaposed to the modern training and standardisation of the gaze. It is through hyperperception as a *form of technology* that it remains a possibility to stay in some authentic relation to the world around us and our emotions. When we arrive at such an instance of unrevealing, we are at the clearing. However, as Heidegger reminded us, it is wise to care for the truth by looking away when it

---

[24] Schirmacher 1999, 6.

is in our vision.[25] Schirmacher proposes that this claim to *forgetting* is a sense that Heidegger borrowed from Nietzsche, who noted that no action would be possible without an ability to forget. This is why the ability to perceive in an extended and enhanced sense would also require the skills of forgetting and abandonment to a larger degree, since the insights and visions that are made available to the perceiver would weigh greater on that person unless it is linked to an ability to unload one's perception. To be effective in practice, it is necessary for an enhanced perceptive ability to be coupled with an extraordinary skill in forgetting and abandonment.

The truth that appears to the beholder is therefore of a character that can only sustain its existence through forgetting. It is in the nature of absence that it is marked by a lack, and this lack can be approached but never completely sutured through techniques of presencing. What could sound somewhat cryptic in Heidegger's formulation, namely that what characterises art is its ability to presence the present, is rendered more approachable and possible to engage in the arts when it is coupled with Schirmacher's notion of hyperperception. It is at the intersection of these concepts that we can begin to grasp in precisely *what* modes the Being as Subject can come to appear to us, and how such an appearance can be rendered by a perceiver that is equipped with the necessary ability to see, feel and forget. In this sense it is a precise echo of Heidegger's notion of *Gelassenheit*: it gives us a sense of how we are held and released into truth as we arrive at a moment of forgetting and abandonment.[26]

We are reminded of Frankl's lessons that our *stance* towards our experiences is what can be the final distinction between our extinction or continued existence. This insight should however be supplemented with the stories of another Jewish inmate of Auschwitz and Buchenwald, the author Imre Kertész, who noted that the horrors of the most modern, efficient and specialized machinery to produce death and suffering invented by human beings – the death camps of the 1940s – also would provide moments of utter happiness:

> You cannot imagine what it's like to be allowed to lie in the camp's hospital, or to have a 10-minute break from indescribable labour. To be very close to death is also a kind of happiness. Just surviving becomes the greatest freedom of all.[27]

The atmosphere of complacency, detachment and engagement in everyday questions is the key to survive camp life in the novels of Kertész. This lesson

---

[25] Heidegger, Discourse on Thinking 1966, 58.
[26] Ibid., 75.
[27] Kandellmarch 2016.

should be forwarded to the hyperperceiver as an antidote and balancing mechanism in the presence of the clearing: forget what you have seen, remain complacent and detached. In such a way you will again receive a sense of blessing and happiness hidden within the forgetting of the presence.

Chapter 4

The art of the rock

In his *About Looking*, John Berger notes how the difference between man and animal lies in that while animals would look at each other in the same way, "only man will recognise this gaze as attentive and wary".[1] Across what Berger refers to as "a narrow abyss of non-comprehension" there is a bridge, and this bridge is unmistakably human. It is when we recognise the familiarity of the animal's gaze: we see ourselves at the moment when we become aware of ourselves.

Already Freud noted, of course, how there is a strict analogy at work between man in his childhood and the childhood of man, i.e., our infantile experiences have their correlate in experiences that was granted to men at the dawn of civilisation.[2] Should not the same logic be extended, so that the recognition we sense in our earliest forefathers is a recognition that has some resonance even in animals that are in some respects similar to us in terms of their ability to perceive and act?

The intervening measure here is related to a sense of culture: as Hegel pointed out, it is only when we acquired an ability to record our laws and our history that our tribal ancestors could achieve a sense of community and belonging that stretched beyond the life of a generation, or, at most, a few generations. Our legal proceedings and journals, our holy scriptures and rituals – these are elements that together are constitutive of a culture, and as a culture it is invested with *traditions*.

What is also true, however, is that our sense of tradition is under pressure from forces that are not strictly within the grasp of any one or any a few of us. These are historical and social mechanisms that have gradually come into effect with modernity and the intensely accelerating socio-economic globalisation that has come to accompany it. The difference with regard to our ability to mediate our natural context through culture is eloquently demonstrated in the way we relate to animals. When cattle first entered our imagination, it was as messengers and prophetic tokens: they could be put to magical, oracular and even sacrificial uses. Only later did cattle come to be associated with milk and meat. With the industrialisation of cattle farming, the last remnants

---

[1] Berger 2009, 1.
[2] Freud, Totem and Taboo 1918.

of the cow as mediator between the holy and the profane has been eradicated: she has now become an irreducible moment in a chain of economic production and reproduction. As Berger notes,

> The 19th century, in Western Europe and North America, saw the beginning of a process, today being completed by 20th century corporate capitalism, by which *every tradition* which had previously mediated between man and nature was broken. Before this rupture, animals constituted the first circle of what surrounded man.[3]

What is crucial here is to take note of the extent to which a relatively recent innovation in the way we organise our societies has led to a total annihilation of a significant and crucial part of our cultural heritage, and that this rupture between ourselves and the creatures that surround us has only been effective for a couple of centuries. In relation to such a short period of time, man was endowing all sort of animals with the strangest, most mythical abilities for a much longer period of our history.

Reason, freedom and the Absolute

The question of what animates our most profound cultural expressions – our arts – was central to Plato, both because of the way this question shows, by way of negation, how we are capable of a kind of reasoning that sets us apart from other beings, and because of the ways in which arts, in Plato's view, were animated in such a way that they could serve to *undermine* the rational governance of the republic.

To address the first issue first, it is clear that Plato perceived the creative act only to be possible when the artist was set aside from himself. It was in a state of being *possessed* that the artwork was made, and while being in possession by the muses, the artist had no sense of his own: no capacity for reason, no ability to apply rational calculation, and so on. Much later the English language philosopher J.L. Austin would propose that our communicative endeavours encompass a number of distinct types: we use symbols to *inform* about and *describe* states of affairs and so on, we use them to *appeal* to others – issue commands, wishes and concessions – so as to convince them to take up the right stance towards a certain issue, and we communicate in order to *express* our sensitivities and exclamations.[4] It is this latter kind of symbolising acts – expressive communication – that is the hallmark of the arts in Plato's view.

---

[3] Berger 2009, 1.
[4] Austin 1962, 1.

The art of the rock

It is in *this* sense that the artist, by way of negation, shows the reasonable underpinnings of our ordinary interaction. The state of excitation and inspiration that enables the artist to create is by the same token the feature that distinguishes him, at the moment of creation, from his fellow citizens. In relation to the inspired artist, we seem rational and sound in our judgement: our ability to distinguish a sensible state of mind from an inspired and possessed position separates us from other beings. It is, Aristotle would later claim, what allows us to refer to ourselves as *rational* animal.[5]

There is a further implication to the artist as inspired and enthused creator of cultural products. To Plato, the original being of an object was solely to be found in the realm of ideas. For instance, while there are many different kinds of carpets being made, collected and used, we can in our minds contemplate an image of the carpet as such, the ideal carpet, so to speak. This wholly imaginary and yet *more real* carpet provides the form for all actually existing carpets that are being made, collected and used. However, unlike the carpet maker who imitates the idea of the carpet to make an actual, usable object, the artist *mimes the imitation.* In other words, the painting or drawing of a carpet is an imitation of an actual object, which itself is an imitation of the idea of carpets. Thus, the artist's depiction of a carpet is twice removed from the ideal, and this further derivation from the form is what made Plato claim that artists are secondary and imitative in their work.[6]

With Austin, we could say that arts have their specificity in that they have no particular *informative* or *instrumental* function in our lives. We cannot usefully sit on a painting, there is little factual information about, say, the French revolution to be drawn from an image, unless it is accompanied by a verbal supplement. Historically, the arts have generally found their place in the service of those who had the resources to fund the creative professions: the church, the dynasts, and, later, wealthy industrialists and financiers. In *this* sense most our artistic tradition has been appellative in nature: it has been put into the service of those who have enabled artists to make art, and

---

[5] Plato, Ion 1892, 501-502. See also Aristotle's *Metaphysics*, book I: "Thus the other animals live by impressions and memories, and have but a small share of experience; but the human race lives also by art and reasoning" (1989, sec. 980b); and book VII, where the distinction is made between universals as necessary, definable substances, and the particularity of attributes, so that, while man can figure as a substance in a Porphyric structure, having a particular attribute is not a part of the thing itself (sec. 1030a). What Porphyry noted was that Aristotle's thinking with regard to substances featured rational as a sub-category of animal, and man as a further sub-division of rational animal.

[6] Plato, The Republic 1888, 307-316. This distinction in Plato is further discussed in the section on inspiration on page 12.

this art has in a more or less explicit way sought to extend the world view of the artist's benefactor.

What is curious about Plato's position on the artist is precisely that it seems to underline *not* the appellative function of arts, but the way they are *expressive* of the artist's mind and emotions. It was *this* characteristic of the arts, and particularly performance arts such as drama that made Plato warn the custodians of the republic against artists and their work. For is it not so, Plato would ask, that a man who has experienced great loss would, or at least should, maintain a subdued and measured relation to his grief? And yet is it no so that on the stage we see characters who, upon losing someone or something dear to them, extol the most bombastic claims, immerse themselves in their grief, and plunge into the depth of misery instead of exercising restraint and calm.[7]

When Plato found that this kind of artistic intervention in the public space could potentially undermine the rational governance of the republic, it is a sentiment that was echoed much later, by the revolutionary dramatist and critic Bertolt Brecht. In opposition to the dominant theatre of his time, which espoused the healing effect of catharsis as the main purpose of drama, Brecht sought to establish a *non-cathartic* theatre, i.e., a drama which did not seek to cleanse its audience of feelings of despair and suffering. Brecht argued that cathartic theatre enabled the societal forms of dominance to continue, since it would allow audiences to find outlets for feelings that were *caused* by social mechanisms in ways that would cement those mechanisms unchanged. Instead, Brecht argued, theatre should highlight those mechanisms as causes of despair and suffering, and, when the play ended, audiences should be invigorated and spurred on in their purposeful abolition of those forms of domination.

In this sense, Plato was right in pointing to the subversive character of the arts, and drama in particular. Theatre can indeed underscore and point to challenges that are unresolved in society, and which can have the effect of changing the way the state is governed, or, indeed, the governance by the state itself. The place for arts and those who made them was therefore clearly *outside* the republic, in Plato's view. Was this a way to stifle criticism of those who governed – a sort of proto-totalitarian state?

What is clear is that Plato's primary target in his derision of the arts is the way the drama tends to exaggerate and dramatise conflicts and suffering,

---

[7] "Then the imitative poet who aims at being popular is not by nature made, nor is his art intended, to please or to affect the rational principle in the soul; but he will prefer the passionate and fitful temper, which is easily imitated?" Ibid., 319-320.

while governance requires an approach to such issues that are more comforting and diplomatic. The question of freedom to express oneself and poetic freedom, in particular, isn't resolved by immediately claiming that any kind of limitation on free speech is an aberration. Think of, for instance, libellous speech or utterances that run counter to the interests of one's own state during a period of conflict, so-called treacherous speech. There are numerous restrictions on our speech, and we accept these limitations without much debate.

In the Middle Ages, poets and artists weren't in high esteem, much along the lines of Plato's general outlook. To the extent that plastic arts and poetry were made it was under the purview of the church and religion. Only with the Renaissance there is a renewed interest in the arts as a singular domain of speech. For John Dryden, it was a matter of delineating a freedom for poetry that was different from the stricture that governed prose. In his essays he noted that poetic

> licence I take to be the liberty which poets have assumed to themselves, in all ages, of speaking things in verse, which are beyond the severity of prose. 'Tis, that particular character which distinguishes and sets the bounds betwixt *oratio soluta* and poetry. This, as to what regards the thought or imagination of a poet, consists in fiction.[8]

To make things up, to create illusions, to delve into fictional universes – these are the things that poets do. The relation between the fictional worlds and the official domain of prose is not entirely clear. It seems as if the imaginative excess Dryden allows for poetic creation leaves open the question of *how* and *what* the fictional poetic universe should relate to our everyday experiences.

Hegel would note how the tragedy remains intimately linked to divinity and religion, even when it has become detached from religious institutions and worship *per se*. Already the Greek tragedy had a mysterious connection with prayer and sacrifice – instituted through the regular events where playwrights showcased their latest work – even when the relation was purely ritual, and with no direct connection to the literal content of religious dogma. To Hegel, the tragedy dramatised substantial forces situated in our will, as

> tragic heroes have their being somehow *beyond* the mere contingency of individuality. They are as if elevated to the work of sculptures, and it is thus that the abstract statues and images of divinities ex-

---

[8] Dryden 1900 [1677], 188-189.

plain more eloquently the high tragic characters of the Greek than any commentary or note.⁹

It is as if we are shown atemporal forces that are connected to our temporal existence through being moulded in rock. To Hegel it was clear that the proper topic of the tragedy was metaphysical, however, it approached its topic in a different way than we find in religious rituals conducted by priests. In the tragedy, metaphysical forces would come down on individual acts, so that the universal substance would manifest itself in earthly matter: "in this form the wilful act and the spiritual substance of its execution constitute the *ethical*".¹⁰ This latter term comes to indicate a metaphysical essence in its temporal domain, so that the drama, in this precise sense, could be said to grant to the audience a form in which the universal would be perceptible.

The connection to Plato's view on the artistic domain is substantiated through Hegel's appropriation of the notion of possession. As with Plato's artist, the tragic individual is governed by, and thus strictly speaking *possessed* by, forces beyond the domain of our immediate grasp. As if becoming the very artwork the tragedy seeks to install, the hero attains a statue-like character, erasing the individuality that constituted the acts and substance behind its endeavours, and so pointing to the *universal* character of its meaning. The tragedy occurs as an effect of the hero's perseverance in a direction that is determined by destiny, which unavoidably unsettles the dust and causes counter-forces to arise:

> The origin of the tragedy consists of the sense in which each side of the contradiction has its *legitimacy* when considered on its own, while they can only put their actual and positive purpose and character through in so far as it constitutes a negation and *bereavement* of the

---

⁹ "In dieser Höhe, auf welcher die bloßen Zufälligkeiten der unmittelbaren Individualität verschwinden, sind die tragischen Helden der dramatischen Kunst, seien sie nun die lebendigen Repräsentanten substantieller Lebenssphären oder sonst schon durch freies Beruhen auf sich große und feste Individuen, gleichsam zu Skulpturwerken hervorgehoben, und so erklären auch nach dieser Seite hin die an sich selbst abstrakteren Statuen und Götterbilder die hohen tragischen Charaktere der Griechen besser als alle anderweitigen Erläuterungen und Noten" (Hegel, Vorlesungen über die Ästhetik 1838, 528).

¹⁰ "In dieser Form ist die geistige Substanz des Wollens und Vollbringens das Sittliche". Ibid., 528, emphasis added.

other, equally justified force and therefore in and through its ethical attitude arrives in a condition of *guilt*.[11]

The contradiction on the level of the individual and singular is resolved on the level of a sense of guilt that is universal and connects the entirety of the field of action. It is in *this* sense we can say that the ethical universe returns in Hegel's view on the tragedy: guilt appears as the quintessential ethical stance in the face of irresolvable, insurmountable contradictions between forces that is manifest on the level of individuals.

The prosaic sense in which the written word and the dramatized encounter remains in a relation of debt to the spoken word and the religious ceremonies that brought it about is supplemented by Dryden's reminder that the poetic word maintains and upholds an original and alienating effect on the audience.[12] When we are in the nearness of poetry, one could say, the universal ethos of the tragedy is reawakened and brought back to life. We are reminded of the *actuality* of the ethical imperative on the tragedy, the limited nature of our capacities, and the work of "thinking, and thereby thanking" in our encounter with the unconcealment of the grace indicated by the tragic.[13]

The specificity of poetry: Miłosz and Ulven

What Dryden made known, as Sir Philip Sydney before him, is that poetry and the poetic deserves a kind of attention and a space of operation that is different from the prose of *doxa* and prescription. The poetic word opens up for a dissimulation of meaning that can have unsettling and inflaming effects on audiences. Plato knew this very well, and his response in *The Republic* would be to recommend its abolition altogether.

---

[11] "Das ursprünglich Tragische besteht nun darin, daß innerhalb solcher Kollision beide Seiten des Gegensatzes für sich genommen *Berechtigung* haben, während sie andererseits dennoch den wahren positiven Gehalt ihres Zwecks und Charakters nur als Negation und *Verletzung* der anderen, gleichberechtigten Macht durchzubringen imstande sind und deshalb in ihrer Sittlichkeit und durch dieselbe ebensosehr in *Schuld* geraten". Ibid., 529. The German *Schuld* translates, a bit roughly, to guilt, although the term also gives associations to indebtedness.

[12] According to Skeat's etymological dictionary, the word *rune*, signifying a character that was cut into stone, derives from Anglo-Saxon *rún*, "a rune, mystery …and lastly a writing, because written characters were regarded as a mystery known to the few". Hence in Icelandic *rún* means secret. The Old High German *rúna*, denoting a secret or a counsel has become the modern *raunen*, to whisper. The base is the Teutonic RÚ-NA, a murmur or whisper (1888, 520).

[13] Heidegger, Discourse on Thinking 1966, 85.

The poetic word is not sufficiently understood unless we situate it in the context of a way of reading that differs from how we read prose. Poetry activates a set of expectations that allow us to ward it off from other domains of speech. For instance, the use of the first-person pronoun in poetry – as in all forms of lyrical deliberation – is not properly decoded as referring to the person who utters it. When we encounter lyrical speech, we recognise this convention and affirm that it is effective by the stance we inhabit as listeners. One way of approaching this discrepancy between the lyrical and the prosaic mode of address is to consider it as a difference in structured expectations.

What was inaugurated by Sydney and Dryden became an acute demand with the new group of writers associated with a novel audience in the wake of modernity in France and Europe. Pierre Bourdieu noted how Gustave Flaubert, in particular, marked the beginning of a way to consider the literary domain as in some crucial senses *different* and *separate* from the rest of culture, and to some extent from the economic world *as such*. Bourdieu's central thesis was that the high cultural field of Flaubert and a host of other literary figures in France in the 19th century obtained a logic that would be best described as "the economic field reversed", so that the more sales and the higher revenue a book would accrue the less it would be recognised as worthy of artistic attention.[14]

The poetic *genre* is crucial here, since volumes of lyrical writing tend to have relatively small audiences and are rarely published in order to provide large revenue for the publisher, but rather with the purpose of improving the kind of recognition the publishing house would receive in society. With the advent of symbolism – such as in the work of Charles Baudelaire – and modernism poetry could be said to manifest in poetic speech the division heralded by Flaubert: from now on poetry would be judged according to standards governed by the poetic community itself, and to be a member of this community meant that one would be in command of a particular form of purchase, what Bourdieu would refer to as *cultural* capital.

The hallmark of modernism is the rupture that is entailed in its dissociation with romanticism and the 19th century social realism. To the modernists it was poetic *effect* that was the primary concern, and the sort of dislocation experience at the turn of the century was to be reconfigured as poetic speech: as fragmented, dissociated and multivoiced as poets experienced the modern encounter should poetry become, and the subject of modernism would be fractured and dishevelled in ways that sought to capture the way life was lived in the 20th century.

---

[14] See Bourdieu 1993.

The art of the rock

To Lithuanian-Polish poet Czesław Miłosz it is the institution of art that serves as the guarantor of a meaning that is relatively fixed and stable in a world of flux and fragmentation. In the poem "The wall of a museum" he describes a world divided by the boundary of the institution of art: on the outside there is rot, garbage, leprosy, poverty and riotous conditions, while, in the inside, there is a friendly silence enveloping a ritual relation to art.[15]

The poem, which can be divided into three parts, goes like this:

> That was an imprinted effigy of a river:
> The flow of a knotty main branch, twigs in confluence,
> As if they wanted to merge,
> Trees and swift water, the best things on earth.
>
> The facade, inlaid with marble panels,
> Towered over a plain of rotting streets,
> Some of them, without end, stretched beyond the horizon,
> Where, in the smoke of garbage cans, in leprous desolation,
> The poor squat, intent on killing each other,
> And, arms ready, police cars make rounds.
>
> When the bus took us to a ritual at the museum,
> We heard beyond the windows yells, jeering,
> Then we were met by smiles and silence.[16]

Each section takes a specific position in relation to the museum. First, we are presented with an imprint, perhaps from the museum's wall. Then, we are given an impression of the world outside the institution, and, finally, we read about the meeting between the narrator or narrators and the institution itself.

This three-tiered structure is central to the meaning of the poem. The image of the river has been carved into material that has preserved it for its aftermath – the time of the poem – and this attempt to capture time is an image of poetry itself. The river flows, like life, and yet the current is not smooth and even: the stream is typically "knotty", like a thought blotched by unresolved questions. The river divides into two branches – a main branch and, we should assume, a minor offshoot – that, of so it seems, come together, "*as if* they wanted to merge". The river becomes a tree, with branches and twigs that have knots. And in all this, we are presented with a question: can a river-tree have desires? It is *as if* the river-tree has a *will* to resolve its knots – to blend its divided and divisive

---

[15] Miłosz 1995, 27.
[16] Blank lines have been added to indicate the three-pronged structure of the poem.

structure – and yet this very trope – the simile – indicates that such a notion would be an imposition. Trees are trees, rivers are rivers, and ascribing volition to such phenomena and objects are anthropomorphisms.

They remain aesthetic entities to us – the onlookers – and it is precisely in the capacity as *exterior* to the writer and reader that they have the potential to provide surplus meaning: the tree as a symbol of life is something we recognise from ancient mythologies, such as the Old Norse *Yggdrasil*, the tree of life, where human beings had their place somewhere in the middle of the tree, between the gods at the tree top and the underworld located beyond the field of visibility. Ferdinand de Saussure, the father of modern linguistics, chose "tree" are the key to open the door to language as a structural phenomenon: while the English "tree" and the French "arbour" can evoke the same or roughly similar thought-images to language-user, their phonemic and graphic differences are ineradicable. The divergence should give us pause to reflect on in what *sense* languages are different. de Saussure's point is that variations on the surface level – the layer of utterance or *parole* – can point to the same deep structure on the level of *langue*. Such is it also with the image of the river and the tree: while they are distinct objects on the level of appearance they share a profound symbolic force: branches, like streams of a river, seem to *relate* in ways that are significant to the onlooker as images of life. The figure resembles Dante Alighieri's from the opening lines of the *Divine Comedy*: mid-way in life a man is confronted with a fork in the road. Which path should he choose? It seems his desire for the diverging paths to merge is wishful thinking: the division is *real*.

Thus is the image *of* the museum *in* the museum: it shows to the onlooker his life and questions him how life should be lived. The second part of the poem asks how life should be *loved*: beyond the marbled exterior of the institution we find "rotting" streets, "smoke of garbage cans", and poor squatters. It is an existence in stark contrast to the "best things on earth" the writer or writers found in the first part. The institution is "towering", we're told, "over" this world of desolation, like a tower that positions itself above and beyond the world it seeks to describe and give proscriptions for. The streets beyond the museum are *not* imprinted in attempts to preserve their being. They are in a state of decay, beyond the singular description granted to the imprint in the poem's opening line: the roads outside the institution come to us as a "plane" – a level – garbled in their nondescript multitude.

Nevertheless, there is a *difference* between the world of the museum and existence beyond it that the poem cannot but acknowledge as putting into play the expanse that separates the material and the immaterial: some roads, decaying as though they are, stretch "beyond the horizon", they are "without end". These *endless* roads are infinite: in contrast to the temporal presence of the rotting streets, the presencing of an atemporal infinitude is another domain of the world outside the institution. It is this *real* of division that lies beyond its boundary: men fight, the have a will, and their desire is to kill each other. The law comes to reinstate order by way of arms at the ready: the police "make rounds", as if the events in the world of squatters if *not* marked by temporal linearity, but by circularity, indicating the recurrence of antagonism on a structural level.

It is as a world shielded from such disharmony and strife that we find the museum. In the third part of the poem we arrive at the institution in the shape of another stark contrast: outside the windows of the bus that took the writer or writers to the museum, there were "yells" and "jeering". Inside the perimeter of the institution, there are "smiles and silence".

The writer or writers – we are never sure which, since it is only in the last part of the text that we are given a pronoun, and it is the plural "we", and it isn't clarified the relation between the "we" of the poem and the instance of writing: did "we" go together to the museum before a single writer wrote the poem or did this "we" also write the poem in unison? – arrives at the institution to attend a *ritual*. Regardless whether this ritual has a formal character or not, the *real* of the divisions *outside* the museum is play-acted or mitigated as dramatic encounter *inside* the institution. The strife and upheaval doesn't go away; it takes a symbolised form.

This is how the institution works: the ritualised *real* of the institution *stands in* for the world beyond its perimeter. What separates the institution from its outside is its walls: they constitute a boundary that is *impenetrable*, even when they're merely structural-symbolic. In short, this is the understanding we should get from psychoanalyst Jacques Lacan's reading of de Saussure's linguistic structuralism: between signifier (sign-image) and signified (the unconscious) stands a bar that *cannot itself be represented*. The *real* of the bar separating the signifier from the signified – the museum from the world it represents – can only be rendered as an open questioning, as silence.

The encounter with man at his dawn as shaped by the experience of modernity is an over-arching presence in the poetry of Tor Ulven. Here, the artistic movement we associate with *modernism* and its particular stance toward *modernity* is postulated both in the sense that art, and poetry in its specificity, should maintain its own relatively autonomous domain in distinction from other cultural forms and from the field of economic relations, and in the peculiar experience brought to life in Ulven's verse: a life world that could only come into existence with the advent of modern knowledge and modern experiences.

Ulven's poetry embarks from a position that is unmistakably surrealist. In his early work, Ulven was interested in the French surrealist movement and translated a collection of poems by Rene Char into Norwegian. When in the

1980s he moved into a more distinctly personal voice, it marked the abandonment of any recognisable social project in his verse. The linkage to political projects that was always present at least as a potentiality with the surrealists no longer serves as a viable matrix of perception to Ulven from *after us, signs* [etter oss, tegn], published in 1980. From then on, his interests are more specifically oriented towards science and the possibilities and limitations that are offered to the kind of knowledge proposed there.

His work at the intersection of archaeology and poetry would yield densely meaningful verse such as this:

That set of teeth
made it out to

the rock's surface
in spite.

The eye's apple, lungs,
Hammurabi's law
stayed in.[17]

Here, the mark of a set of teeth is made visible on the surface of a rock, an object that would be of interest to archaeologists, while those elements that we associate with the teeth – eyes, lungs, and so on – have *not* been inscribed into the rock: for them to reach the level of imprint it is necessary with the poetic remainder. In one sense, Ulven's poem draws our attention to those biological components that are not present in the archaeological sign, and, in another, we become aware of the work of poetry in resuscitating those signs that demand the work of imagination to become present.

It is for these reasons that the introduction of Hammurabi's law in the penultimate stanza of the poem becomes meaningful in an extraordinary way. First, it transcends the merely biological and inorganic matter that is available *as* rock and *on* the rock. Second, it introduces the element of culture to the biological necessity implied by first elements of the poem. And finally, the law that remains – i.e., that is *not* placed on the outside – is an artefact in its own

---

[17] Den tanngarden der
trasset seg ut til overflaten
av steinen. Øyeeple, lunger,
Hammurabis lov ble inne.
From the collection *Patient* [Det tålmodige], first published in 1987 (Ulven 2001, 169, author's translation).

right: the legal order that is constitutive of society has its precise analogy in the order of poetry that finds its expression in the poetic as such.

This is why the short poem by Ulven is a poetic programme in miniature: the law of expression and poetry has remained on the inside of order from the set of teeth made their mark on the rock itself. It is an unchanging and persistent character of art and culture that is brought out in Ulven's poem: is it not as if we can hear the sound of the archaic, ritual shaman exclaim the genesis of the tribe itself?

The notion that organic and biological matter actualise the potentiality of inorganic rocks are apparent in many places in Ulven's work. For instance, in a poem from *Garbage Sun* (1989) he notes how we can get the feeling of approaching the state of rocks when we roam restlessly at night:

(Giacometti: *Tête sur tige*)

Finally
a man
wakes

like the rock's
potentiality
to scream.[18]

Ulven's poem conveys a sense in which we experience the *arrival* of a moment that has been promised. The time has arrived "at last" when man has been able to fulfil the promise of the rock, which is nothing less than the ability to scream.

The key verb in the first stanza, *vake*, has a range of possible meanings in the Norwegian. It could indicate the state of being awake, such as when we lie awake or stay awake during times of distress. It could also point to a state of confusion as if denoting a person that drifts around without aim and without any sense of direction of purpose. Finally, it could signify the movement we associate with fish when they hover around a particular area: fishermen would ask each other where they should go to find fish that *vaker*.

---

[18] "Endelig
vaker
et menneske som steinens
evne til
skrik"
Ibid., 203, author's translation.

The character in the poem seems to have been reduced to the immediacy of animals: drifting around senselessly, as we sometimes do when we have stayed awake beyond our capacities, unable or unwilling to sleep for some reason or other. It is only in the second stanza that this biological existence is further reduced, as we saw in the example for *Patience*, to the level of inorganic matter. It is the rock's potentiality to communicate that has found its outlet in the sleepless drifter.

Can the rock communicate? Is the scream uttered by the poem's persona an intentional statement or should we understand it as an expression of agony and suffering? If the latter is the case, it is as if it is the essence of our existence to search for outlets for these kinds of inchoate howls.

The encounter between people in Ulven's poetry is consequently closer to the kind of meeting we would expect when we come across inorganic matter. It isn't clear whether there are other people in Ulven's poetry at all: at most, they seem to linger as memories or remnants of potentialities that remain unrealised. When Ulven's poetic subject looks into the eyes of others he sees nothing but ghosts:

> I see death
> everywhere.
>
> It's in
> the eyes.
> The gaze is rotten. Sharp.
> Non-political.[19]

The image of the first stanza – a person who sees nothing but death – is juxtaposed with a meeting with other people in the second. However, the death that the subject sees everywhere turns out to be characteristic precisely of the encounter he has with others: it is something he recognises in their gaze. This is why, he explains, their gaze is rotten: it has the cadaverous mark of mortality, and the kind of clairvoyance we can expect from someone who has already passed into the realm of the dead can be nothing but apolitical.

---

[19] "Jeg ser døden
overalt. Den sitter
i øynene.
Blikket er råttent. Klart.
Upolitisk. "
From the collection *Garbage Sun* [Søppelsolen], first published in 1989. Ibid., 223, author's translation.

Conceptual art and the return to philosophy

When it is noted that conceptual art is a movement within the history of art that has not yet been fully appreciated, this is due to the double break provided by those artists operating within the parameters of the *concept* from the 1960s and onwards.[20] They went beyond the purely formal and syntactical interrogations of the tradition that was inaugurated by painters such as de Kooning, Kandinsky, Rothko and others, so that, with the conceptual artists, it is no longer merely a question of what the formal *frames* are for what should be properly considered a painting, or how a painting need to articulate a set of inherited elements of expressive *grammar* in order to receive recognition from the world of art. In addition, conceptual art took as its matter a whole new domain of notions: from now on it would become possible to interrogate questions that had hitherto been the purview of intellectual inquiry. Conceptual art brings up the question of the intellect and the philosophical act in a whole new way as a mode of artistic expression.

To reawaken Heidegger's approach to the artwork, we could say that conceptual art seeks to bring to the fore the *concept-ness* or conceptuality of the concept. In his commentary on van Gogh's painting of a pair of worn-out shoes, Heidegger would note that the plastic arts had a particular ability to show a truth about a visual reconfiguration that could only take place in the arts. It is when we come into the nearness of the artwork as such that we can begin to experience the unconcealment of the specific truth embedded in the plasticity of the work, and this encounter between the work and the audience should be considered an *event* that unfolds as we are drawn into the orbit of art, and that withdraws as the artwork retreats from our attention.

The attempt to bring closer together the various modalities of art that we find, for instance, in the work of Richard Wagner – the so-called *Gesamtkunstwerk* – should be regarded as a precursor to conceptual art. It would include a whole range of musical, plastic and performing arts brought to the attention of an audience with the view of providing a total experience of art. However, the limitation to Wagner's kind of total art was that it remained embedded in view of the arts as fundamentally narrative and enveloped in tradition. Conceptual arts are not inherently committed to any of those moments: they are more interested in ideas and questions than stories, and they can take any kind of material, or even *non-material*, object as their ground.

---

[20] Schellekens 2014.

Figure 4.1: The Weather Project - Olafur Eliasson, The Weather Project (2003).

Two recent examples should give us a rough idea of the outlook provided by conceptual arts. First, in the work of Olafur Eliasson there is a persistent attention to how images and installations can trigger questions and interrogations that we tend to associate with the domains of *philosophy* and *critical inquiry*. For instance, in his 2003 installation at the Tate Modern in London, Eliasson made use of an entire factory hall to display a large, beaming sun (see figure 4.1).[21] The ceiling was covered with a mirror, so that audiences coming into the hall could observe themselves – as tiny, miniature reflections – as inverted figures above their heads. What happened was that the hall became a lounge area, where guests at the gallery would sit down, relax and communicate. It was as if

---

[21] Eliasson 2003.

Eliasson had indeed recreated an outdoor space complete with sun and a comfortable atmosphere. The major incursion was the mirror in the ceiling, as if the artwork would say to the audience: remember to reflect on the reflection.

Figure 4.2: Come back Muse - Sigurður Gudmundsson, "Come back Muse" (2013).

A second example, by Sigurður Gudmundsson, is provided by a photographic image: a shaven man's head, painted in blue, with a horizontal white line, is depicted *en face* facing a small bush or tree (see figure 4.2).[22] The man's face is contorted into a scream so that it is as if he is directing his scream to the tree. The primordial setting is unmistakable: our burst of incommunicable noise against the conditions of existence here takes the figure of a man, reduced to a hairless, screaming head, in a pre-linguistic agony directed toward the very object that could provide him with shelter from the shifting climatic conditions, that could provide him with food, and that could be a source of wood for heating. The allegorical representation of man's existential condition is doubled by the reference it gives to the notion of signification and provision of meaning we find in the founding text of modern linguistics: in Ferdinand de Saussure's *Course in General Linguistics* it is precisely the tree (or *arbour* as it's French

---

[22] Gudmundsson 2013.

counterpart) that stands as the key signifier that comes to symbolise the entire field of signification. It is, as it were, the root of de Saussure's system.[23]

In Gudmundsson's photograph, de Saussure's distinction between signifier (the audible or visible referent) and signified (that which is referred to) is rendered as paint on the head. However, in this instance, the signifier and signified bears no mark of difference: it is the same colour blue that covers each side of the bar that divides the sign, as if in the scream the referent and the referee come together as sign and meaning, without distinction. What does remain of the sign-structure is the bar itself. In the words of Jacques Lacan, what we learn from the teaching of de Saussure is that between the signifier and the signified there is a bar *that cannot itself be represented.*[24] In other words, the bar indicates the system itself: an insurmountable distinction that enables us to grasp the way man's communication is different from cries of the instinctual drives. What Gudmundsson's photographic image shows us is how there is a remnant to meaning that eludes us so that it is through the encounter with the work of art that this surplus meaning can become tangible.

The notion that art could become a vehicle for ideas, devoid of any material or physical ground, becomes a highly charged moment in the work of conceptual artist Robert Barry.[25] His *Closed Gallery* (1969) consisted solely of invitations to various gallery shows, stating that "During the exhibition the gallery will be closed". Another example is provided by his *Telepathic Piece* (1969), where he stated that "During the exhibition I will try to communicate telepathically a work of art, the nature of which is a series of thoughts that are not applicable to language or image". What is clear from these examples is how conceptual art, through reflecting on itself as art, detaches itself from any tangible material form, literally standing in for the idea – or *concept* – itself.

One case where Barry would make use of de Saussure's distinction between signifier and signified is his *Inert Gas Series*, where a poster would announce the artwork, accompanied by an address (a PO box in Los Angeles) and a tele-

---

[23] Saussure 1983.
[24] Evans points out that Lacan first makes use of the term bar to indicate the line that separates signifier from signified in de Saussure's algorithm, so that it shows the resistance that is provided in signification. It is a bar that can only be crossed through metaphor. The French word for bar, *barre*, is an anagram of *arbre* (tree), which is de Saussure's metaphoric representation of the sign itself (1996, 15). The non-representativity of the bar itself comes out clearly in Seminar VI, where Lacan claimed that "what man leaves behind him is a signifier, it is a cross, it is a bar, qua barred, qua overlaid by another bar which indicates …that as such it has been effaced" (from the unpublished transcript of Lacan's lecture on Lacan, December 10, 1958, see also 1982, 11-52).
[25] Bull 2015.

The art of the rock 79

phone number. By calling the phone number audiences would hear an answering machine describing the work: Barry's venture into the desert to release inert gases into the atmosphere. As Malcolm Bull notes, what we have here is a separation of "the release of the gases (invisible and virtually inaccessible) and its presentation as an ephemeral audio recording and a publicity poster".[26] The exhibition had become an instance of "pure sign", without material foundation: it was a concept that audiences would have to give their imaginary contribution so as to exist.

The successive stripping away of elements that are not strictly necessary for the conceptual content of the artwork to appear is an approach that would be strongly present in the poetry of Tor Ulven.[27] By moving from consciousness to biological existence, Ulven emphasised the instinctual and psychological components that undergird our experience of the world, and this appeal to our common denominator would appear even more forcefully when he further devolved the poetic gaze to encounter the rock itself: in the poem on Giacometti man's consciousness is reduced to a biological drive that finds its outlet in a scream, which should be interpreted as the howl of the rock itself.

Reducing consciousness to drive, and further extrapolating inorganic matter from biological impulses invites us to ask what such a common denominator could be: are we not, it seems pertinent to ask, confronted with the physical minimal entity itself, the atom, as it were, that lies at the core of the rock, as much as the life that inhabits it? However, and this is the key point that places Ulven at a distance to physicalism and other forms of materialist art, the stripping away of elements in his work does not stop at the atom: as was the case with conceptual art, Ulven would show us how the notional content of art arrives only *after* all physical substrata has been effectively laid bare, and audiences are confronted with their ability to make meaning out of the remnants of a bare structure.

In an essay on "The infinity of Leopardi", Ulven noted how the essential component of art consists in its "appeal to something infinitely different, while the artwork itself remains (by necessity) limited, and this limitation is what art leaves to our imagination to fill in and supplement beyond limits".[28] This act of pointing to, or, as Hegel would have it, *elevating* our individual experience into an existence that is heroic in its sculpted appearance – in other words, indicating the absolute – is something that becomes tangibly

---

[26] Ibid., 93.
[27] It is a way of engaging with the content matter that is also forcefully present in his more prose oriented works, such as the novel *Succession* [Avløsning] (1993), a text that elaborates some 30 consciousnesses that succeed each other as narrators and focalisers.
[28] Ulven, Essays. 1997, 89.

present when Ulven would ask us to reflect on the essence of art. By allowing poetry to treat other art forms as subjects, Ulven indicates the tragic and unavoidable universality that governs art and out experience of the rock. In a commentary on a sculpture – easily imaginable as one of Alberto Giacometti's ultra-slim figures – Ulven proposes the following scene from a park:

raindrops

on the protruding
underarm, chin
nipple

of a sculpture:
running
hanging

before falling, water swarming.
immovable
sculpture.

you do not bolt your forehead
against the bronze, just
watching.

the green park
closed.[29]

---

[29] "Regndråpene på den fremstikkende
underarmen, på
hakespissen
og brystvorten til en skulptur:
de triller
og henger før de faller. Vannet myldrer.
Skulpturen urørlig. Du dunker ikke pannen
mot bronsen. Du bare
ser. Parken
er grønn
og stengt."
First printed in *That which has no value – Selected poems* (1993) (2001, 243, author's translation).

Chapter 5

Particles and universals

The age old debate between hermeneutics and transcendence in the way we approach truth and meaning found a pithy formulation in Mike Leigh's film *Naked*, where the picaresque anti-hero comments that it seems wasteful to plunge into the depths of space to pry out the secrets of our world, when we have not yet come to terms with our existence *down here*.[1] Is the *truth out there* or *down here*? As we shall see in this chapter the answer is both: what we consider to be out there is premised on how we comport ourselves down here and what we disclose of the world out there has effects on our lives.

The challenges to Copernicus' heliocentric world-view have been apparent for at least a century: the notion of relativity and the realisation that we cannot determine an object's position *and* movement without abandoning the precision with which we specify the value of either has caused some debate with regard to the possibility of any firm ground for knowledge and truth. In the first section of this chapter we shall investigate three such challenges: multiverse theory and its effects on the way we perceive our astronomical and psychic domains; the Heisenberg theorem and its reconfiguration of our understanding of the position and movement of particles, as well as its implications for our existential space; and recent arguments concerning distributions of spacetime and matter to cover the manifold of events, and how they invite us to question the foundation of the universe we navigate.

One pathway into the unconscious – apart from our daily neurotic encounters with the world – is through what the French call the *passage to the act* and the ways in which the subject can cause a rupture in the fabric that limits and constrain his existence. Beyond and against the current idea of applauding a state of melancholy psychoanalysis poses a break with the depressed form of

---

[1] Leigh 1993. The film shows the underbelly of a London that is no longer fit for its heroes: the main character, colourfully portrayed by David Thewlis, quotes vividly from works of philosophy, sociology, holy scriptures, and so on. Leigh has remarked in an interview that what characterises him is that he is "a reader. He's one of those kids teachers have turned away from because their intelligence is too unruly" (Jeffries 2008).

attachment through an outburst of activity.² This active phase takes us beyond our initial sense of shock when we are wounded, or the fictional framework that has maintained our sense of self is seriously threatened. What the *passage to the act* does is to provoke a reaction from the instance Jacques Lacan referred to as the big Other: the law and its caretakers. We are made to realise our limits, and the constraint put in place by the forces of order can have the effect of further pressing us down into feelings of melancholy and *tristesse*. The second section of this chapter seeks to find a way of this impasse: tracing the analytic encounter through its phases of identifying symptoms as compromise-formations, through transversal of fantasies, to the pass from analysis to analyst, the rôle of fetishes, aggression and feelings of destitution is examined to show how the analyst relies on a sense of separation, lack of causality and a rigorous objectivity in rendering desire.

The third section traces the rhetorical strategy of irony as it was employed by Socrates to acquire a voice in the choir of power. However, as Søren Kierkegaard noted, the negativity of irony, its deceit, and undercutting of existential meaning contributed to Socrates' own death warrant. Against this strategy, Kierkegaard proposes the heroic stance of John in his rendition of Christ: a depiction that can, finally, only be achieved as silence.

Across the multiverse

It is possible that we can construct a spaceship and use it to travel to a different place where we could encounter other beings that are recognisably conscious, human-like or in the least have the ability to register sensations. Simple mathematical probabilities show that we already have within our grasp the very likely possibility that there are indeed parallel universes and that they are inhabited with beings like ourselves.³

For this notion of multiverse to be true, it is necessary that we assume space to be unlimited, or at least sufficiently large, to contain constellations of matter that reoccur about every 10 to 1028 metres, and that space is more or less uniformly filled with matter. Our limitation with regard to this

---

² When considered as laudable emotions in popular culture, melancholy and sadness can work as fetishes that bar the subject from moving beyond attachments that it experiences as alienating. The psychoanalytic distinction between alienation and separation reveals how the former feeds on anxiety associated with a sense of having been made not to belong in our former place of residence. Against this, separation is what occurs when the subject relinquishes the bond to the homestead. The associated emotion here is not anxiety, but despair: it is what the hysteric endures at the transversal of the phantasy that sustained his or her melancholy (Stevens 2007, Žižek, Da Capo senza Fine 2000, 253).
³ Tegmark 2003.

version of multiverse theory is our sense of *sight*. Today we can only see about 4 x 1026 metres into space, which amounts to what is referred to as a Hubble volume. If we assume unlimited space, each universe will have a range of vision equal to ours, defined around their planets. If space is infinite, there will be an infinite number of planets where an infinite range of events – even the most improbable – take place.

This vision is based solely on statistics and the idea that space is infinite. As Max Tegmark notes, there are sufficient observational data to support the view that matter *is* uniformly distributed in space, so that this notion of multiverse, based as it is on a model of physics that predates quantum mechanics, seems trivially obvious. While Albert Einstein did speculate that space could be finite or limited if it has an unusual shape, say formed like a donut, a pretzel or a sphere – such topologies have no edges and a limited volume – studies of the microwave background indicate that space is not finite: the hot and cold spots that have been observed are simply too small to support the idea that space has a spherical topology.

Even if we cannot observe our siblings in a parallel universe, probabilities have it that they are there, have the same experiences as us, considering the same options as we do, and suffering from the same deprivations as us. To put the matter in psychoanalytic terms, what seems true in physics is that there are subjects who have the same encounters with their life-worlds, who are torn apart at every moment by their difference with respect to the choices they make. In the view of Jacques Lacan, the division of the subject of analysis from his or her closest relations is an effect of the intervention of the Other.

We see this separation most distinctly in Lacan's *schema L* (figure 5.1).

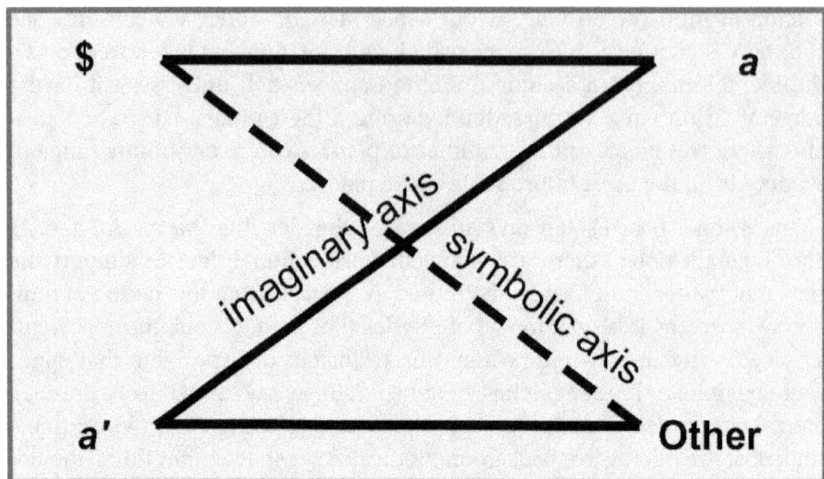

Figure 5.1: Schema L - Lacan's Schema L. Note that the terms on the imaginary axis (a and a') are reversed in his seminar on psychosis.[4]

Here, the analysand is enabled to separate his or her life-world from that of his parallel cousins through the work of analysis. To put it differently, analysis makes for the analytic subject a sense of the I that repositions itself in relation to the (small) other – our parallel universe cousins – so as to facilitate a life world that is distinctly different. The work of analysis enables us to perceive the other as an inhabitant of a different universe and to reinforce our sense of inhabiting our own world.

With the introduction of quantum mechanics, ascertaining the location and movement of a particle becomes even acuter. Werner Heisenberg sought to reduce the complexities of approaching sub-atomic particles' position and velocity by introducing two limitations to quantum physics: it should *only* consider events that were observable, and it should regard the *meaning* of an event as commensurable with its measurability. However, even within these strict boundaries, Heisenberg encountered insurmountable difficulties in determining the position and velocity of a particle: the more precise our knowledge of the *state* of a system, the more diffuse our knowledge of its *velocity*, and vice versa.

Are the challenges in ascertaining a system's state and velocity through the same experiment due to a shortfall in our measuring apparatuses, to some inadequacy in the observer, or is it a characteristic of the essential connection of particles and waves? The answer to this question should be approached

---

[4] Lacan, Seminar on 'The purloined letter' 2006, 40, On a question prior to any possible treatment of psychosis, 458.

Particles and universals

through an understanding of what Einstein referred to a "principle theories", i.e., theories that take as their departure observations in order to deduce theories of the physical world. [5] In a single quantum system, the uncertainty understood as the probability distribution, of measurement results, is attributed to the initial state of the system. However, it is more typical to consider the following experimental situation:

1. Prepare one and only one quantum system.

2. Couple this single quantum system to an unknown force.

3. Introduce a second quantum system – a probe – into the test system and measure the observables (e.g., position and velocity).

4. Repeat steps 2 and 3 in order to determine a dependent unknown force.

While Heisenberg in his original formulation considered the uncertainty principle as a way to approach measurement error and so-called back action (i.e., noise resulting from the finite pulse duration of a single photon) related to the probe, there are more common in quantum theory today to consider that uncertainty also applies to the initial quantum system. This initial uncertainty is often referred to as "lack of causality" in quantum measurements.[6]

In Heisenberg's first formulation the uncertainty principle is an epistemological concern. He would state that "the more precisely the position [of an electron] is determined, the less precisely the momentum is known, and conversely".[7] However, from the claim that this principle limits what we can *know*, Heisenberg would propose that the principle applies to the very definition of concepts: in so far as an experiment could provide definitions for one

---

[5] Einstein distinguished between constructive and principle theories. While the former "build a picture of complex phenomena out of some relatively simple proposition", principle theories "employ the analytic, not the synthetic method. Their starting point and foundation are not hypothetical constituents, but empirically observed general properties of phenomena, principles from which mathematical formula are deduced of such a kind that they apply to every case which presents itself" (Einstein 1919, 41, Lange 2014). See also Hilgevoord, Jan, and Jos Uffink 2006, sec. 2.4.

[6] "Die Quantenmechanik die Ungültigkeit des Kausalgesetzes definitiv festgestellt" (Heisenberg 1927, 197).

[7] "Je genauer der Ort bestimmt ist, desto ungenauer ist der Impuls bekannt und umgekehrt" (ibid., 175).

quantity (say, position), it would be subject to indeterminacies which would prohibit it from providing a simultaneous definition of, say, velocity.[8]

The ambiguity of Heisenberg's own approach to his principle reveals the sense in which uncertainty operates on the border between *knowledge* and *truth*. On the one hand, our drive to find and catalogue a totality of knowledge entices us to seek out a formulation of quantum theory that would give certainty on a simultaneous measurement of conjugate qualities (e.g., position and velocity). However, our sense of truth reveals that the drive has its limitation, and this boundary effect is achieved by its tendency to seek its own extinction. Truth, then, is the property of a domain that lies beyond the psychoanalytic concept of drive: it is the world made meaningful to man, an animal that is able to signify and consider his own sense of existence.

What the hole argument does is to pose another question of those who claim there to be a *literal* reading that should serve as the realist foundation of physics. The argument starts from the fusion of space and time into a single concept, spacetime, in modern physics, and then goes on to ask if it is reasonable to claim that spacetime exists independently of the processes occurring within it.[9] This view is referred to as spacetime substantivism, since it assumes spacetime to be a substance in and of itself. What the hole argument shows is that when a theory, such as Einstein's general theory of relativity, has *more* maths than its correlate physical reality, such an excess – known as *gauge freedom* – can only be determined by some physical ground. If a theory is held up by such an excess of properties that neither verification nor logical analysis can decide its viability, then it's time to consider a different perspective.

The general covariance of Einstein's general theory of relativity entails that geometrical structures can be distributed across a manifold of events in a number of ways. In two distributions, the events are left unaltered while the metric field, which specifies properties such as an event's temporal and spatial relation to other events, and the matter field, representing the matter of the universe, are transformed so that it appears as if there is a hole in the structure:

---

[8] See Hilgevoord, Jan, and Jos Uffink 2006, sec. 2.2.
[9] Norton 2015.

Particles and universals 87

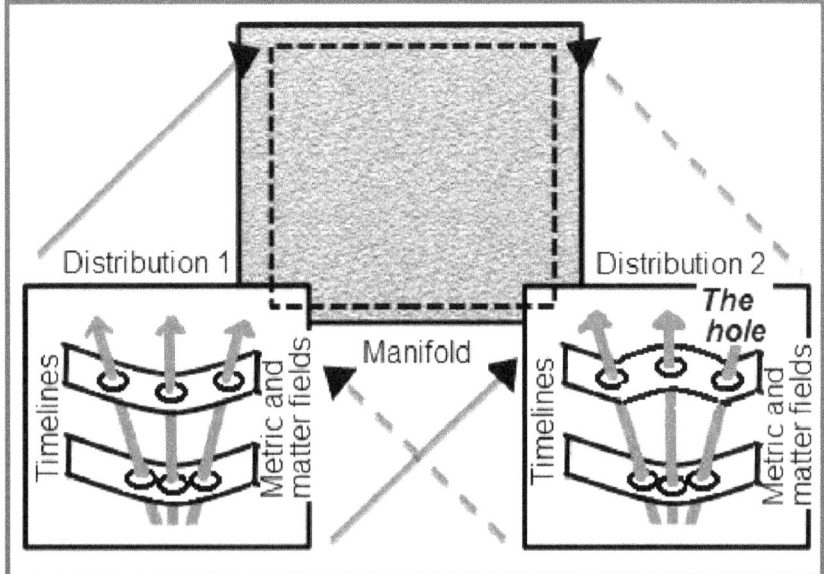

Figure 5.2: Distributions - Two ways to spread metric and matter over a manifold of events.

The key is that the hole transformation leaves the fields outside the hole unchanged while they are spread differently *inside* the hole, and the spreadings inside and outside the hole are joined smoothly. The two distributions are in full agreement on all invariant properties, which is to say that they cannot be distinguished through observation.

When we assign metrical and material properties differently to the manifold of events, the substantivalist would claim that we are now operating with two physically distinct possibilities. As John D. Norton notes, "manifold substantivalists must deny an equivalence inspired by Leibniz...: if two distributions of fields are related by smooth transformation, then they represent the same physical system".[10]

However, the distributions are both equally permissible extensions of the metric and matter fields, since they both agree with the laws of the theory. Therefore, the theory cannot decide if only one of the distributions should be admitted.

The hole argument claims that substantivalists ascribe an unwarranted repertoire of properties to spacetime in order to salvage the claim that the

---

[10] Ibid., sec. 5.

two distributions should be regarded as two distinct systems, that the doctrine should be regarded.

While realists tend to read the general theory of relativity literally – claiming that there *really is* a manifold of events and metrical structure such as it is described by the theory – the hole argument sets out to refute the literalists on the basis of the excessive properties that have to be assigned to the posited in order to maintain the position, and which can nevertheless not be verified nor determined by the laws of the theory.

The shift from a literal to a more ambiguous approach to a set of events has its precise correlate in the psychoanalytic transformation from decidability to metaphor. The movement is structured by the subject's entry into the symbolic order: from a being that is wholly determined by the psychoanalytic drives, the subject receives the ability to relate to the world through a metaphoric symbolisation. To Jacques Lacan, the metaphor was the hallmark of our articulation of desire. Metaphors are indicative of a gap between the literal usage and the figurative employment of speech that is possible after we have become subject to sexuation: when we have realised the boundary imposed by the phallic function we can become desiring subjects, and as such we start our navigation in the world of metaphor displacement.

Passages

The sense in which the subject of analysis goes through a *passage* at the completion of the treatment is a figure that would become central to the work of Lacan. The term *passage à l'acte* – passage to the act – is derived from French jurisprudence, where a purportedly criminal act committed under this rubric absolves the perpetrator of civil responsibility.[11] In clinical psychiatry it is used to designate impulsive acts of a criminal or violent nature, marking the point where the subject moves from a violent idea or intention to the corresponding act.

What is clear is that Lacan would use the term passage also to designate a different transposition, namely the passage (*passe*) that constitutes the final moment of the analytic process. This passage is what marks the shift of "analysand into analyst", and it is the moment when the desire of the analyst is turned into "desire in its pure state".[12] The double meaning of the term in Lacan's terminology is not arbitrary: as the passage of the act stands for the moment when an unbearable thought is transformed into an act, the passage of the analysis marks the transformation of analysis itself and its finality. In

---

[11] Evans 1996, 136.
[12] Žižek, The undergrowth of enjoyment 1999, 32.

this sense, the term passage can stand as a token for the entirety of Lacan's approach to symptomatic rendering.

The analysis can be distilled into three distinct formulae, which succeeds each other as the completion of one marks the onset of the other. First, the identification of symptoms has as its purpose to enable the analysand to get rid of them as compromise-formations. Here, it is instructive to consider the fetish as symptomatic of what we could call a melancholic form of attachment. Slavoj Žižek has noted the elevated status emotions such as sadness and melancholy has achieved in our culture, and in our approach to these affects it is necessary to consider their relation to the lost love-object. Melancholy, Žižek claims, is the fetishisation of the incomplete detachment from this object, so that the object isn't really lost, it is only absent to the subject, who can persist in his or her refusal to accept the loss. In this way, melancholy and sadness indicate a state of *alienation*, and should be clearly distinguished from *separation*, which occurs when we have affirmed the loss and no longer seek out states of sadness.

In a more abstract sense, fetishes are in themselves symptoms of incomplete detachments: they operate as means by which the subject can continue to fantasize about a state where the love-object isn't really lost. It is in this context we should understand the psychoanalytic notion of sadism, which, as Jan Wiener remarks, should be distinguished from aggression.[13] Aggression situates the subject as intent on pursuing its own survival, and so that it figures as a way to counter what the subject perceives as an existential threat. In this sense, the subject employs it as a protective measure and disregards any effect it has on others. Sadism, on the other hand, is the wish to inflict physical or mental suffering on others, and the fetish arises from the sexualised pleasure that would arise from such infliction of pain.

It is useful to take a historical perspective on sadism in the psychoanalytic tradition. Already the pre-Freudians were deeply engaged in a debate over the pathological status of this kind of sexualised joy experienced as a result of others' suffering. Richard von Krafft-Ebing designated "the desire to cause pain to the sexual object and its opposite", i.e., the desire to cause pain to oneself, as two forms of pleasure in suffering: sadism as its active form, and masochism a passive expression.[14] Other authors prior to Freud used one term to designate both forms, *algolagnia*. Freud noted how von Krafft-Ebing's terms foregrounded "the pleasure secured in all kinds of humility and submission", whether to oneself or others. Today, sadism and masochism are more often regarded as a – sometimes legitimate – sexual fetishes, with their own associations, places of

---

[13] Wiener 1998, n.4.
[14] See Freud, Three Contributions to the Theory of Sex 1930, 21-23.

meeting, magazines, etc. [15] As a fetish – whether we regard it in its gaze inherited from Freud and his precursors, i.e., as a pathology, or in today's more accepting and inclusive environment – it works to hide the incomplete detachment from the love-object. Therefore, when Freud noted that the sadism and, later, masochism, expressed by the child in his essay on "A child is being beaten" is an infantile articulation of sexual desire, it was with the view that *algolagnia* is a form of pleasure we tend to grow out of.[16] To Freud, when we encounter such pleasures in adults, it should be considered pathological.

While sadism and masochism constitute examples of fetishes that are *symptomatic* of an incomplete separation from the lost love-object, anger is an emotion we encounter as an effect of the loss itself. Fetishes serve as compromises in our engagement with desire, and the first step of analysis would be to identify and leave behind these formations. However, what we encounter as a result is the fantasmatic frame that upholds the co-ordinates of our enjoyment.

Thus, the second analytical step is to transverse such fantasies. It is during this phase that anger reveals the subject's experience of being threatened, i.e., it functions as a counter-index of fantasmatic transversal. In Lacan's perspective on the psyche, fantasies are necessary, albeit fictional, mechanisms of defence that we develop as we move from an image of the body that is fragmented and inchoate to a sense of our physical frame that Lacan characterised as "orthopaedic".[17] When we arrive at a self-perception that constitutes a veritable fortress of alienating identity, our former body image returns only as nightmarish images of persecution and as limbs detached from the body. These are hysterical interventions in an already established *I* formation, and as such, they are distinctively different from the symptoms of the neurotic, who seeks to re-establish the fortress of the ego through mechanisms such as inversion, isolation, reduplication and (metaphorical) displacement.[18]

Lacan's approach to the term fantasy is therefore crucially different from the view we generally take on it, since in this psychoanalytic approach, fantasies are necessary for the constitution of the *I*. Without such a fantasmatic support, the ego loses its foundation, and the subject is thrown back into the hysterical universe of the fragmented imaginary. This is why it makes sense to say that for Lacan, behind the unravelling of a fantasy we will find another fantasy: they are

---

[15] Sadomasochism as a sexual fetish – so-called BSDM – is considered a legal and non-pathological form of enjoyment in, among other places, the Scandinavian countries, Germany, Netherlands and Austria, under certain well-defined circumstances.
[16] See Freud, 'A child is being beaten': a contribution to the study of the origin of sexual perversions 1919, 175-204.
[17] Lacan, The mirror stage as formative of the I function 2006, 78.
[18] Ibid., 78-79.

illusions we simply cannot live without. The possible *transversal* of a fantasy should not be considered as having the aim of ridding the subject of any possible fantasmatic support – and so as, as social realists might contend, to usher us into the uncompromising reality of existence – but, rather, to cross the boundary that barricades us in isolation from any tactile relation to the world.

It is in this context that we should understand anger as a means for the subject to counter what is experienced as an existential threat. When the fantasy is transversed, it involves "our *over-identification* with the domain of imagination: in it, through it, we break the constraints of the fantasy and enter the terrifying, violent domain of pre-synthetic imagination, the domain in which *disjecta membra* float around, not yet unified and 'domesticated' by the intervention of the homogenizing, fantasmatic frame".[19] The notion of transversal conjured by Žižek closely resembles a state described by Lacan as hysterical: it simulates the pre-symbolic imaginary where bodies are detached from their limbs (Žižek's *disjecta membra*), and the stabilising defences of the ego have been overrun in an attempt to push the subject into an experience of horror and violence. Is it not reasonable for the analysand to respond with anger in this context? When we are treated to images created to frighten us and to instill in us a world that is violent and incoherent, it appears to be a measured response to answer with a reestablishment of the perimeter of the ego.

What is clear is that Lacan would distinguish clearly between anger as a form of agitation – the kind of acting out as a way to communicate with the big Other – and the violence we associate with the passage to the act.[20] In the two latter cases, we are in the domain of anxiety, and the *symptom* is what bars the subject from *acting out* a message to the Other. Thus, when we move from the first phase of analysis, which involved the identification and elimination of the symptom, we are already at the threshold of the kind of aggression that we find in the domain of a subject who *acts out*. Acting out is therefore symptomatic of the transversal of a fantasmatic frame – the second phase of analysis – in so far as it is counter-indicative of its dissolution. This type of aggression works as a "hidden" message to the big Other: "I stand by your law, however, in this particular situation I have no choice but to violate its content so as to demonstrate the threat to which the law has been exposed".

If acting out was an option that was barred from the subject as long as it was enveloped in the symptom, the passage to the act is what disables the analysand's access to his or her experience of *anguish*, despair and destitution. It is

---

[19] Žižek, Is it possible to traverse the fantasy in cyberspace? 1999, 122.
[20] See Stevens 2007, 148, Evans 1996, 136-137.

here that we truly arrive at the possibility of the existential encounter with the analysand's experience of truth. As Søren Kierkegaard noted,

> Despair [is] sickness unto death, this horrifying contradiction, this illness in the soul, forever to die, to die and yet not to die, to die death. Thus to die entails that it is over, but to die death means to experience dying; and if *this* can be experienced for a single moment, then it is so as to by the same token forever have it as experience. [21]

This experience of death as a component of life can only be obtained through the passage that Lacan formulates as the exit from the symbolic network.[22] When the subject in this manner seeks to dissolve the social bond, he or she is no longer a communicating agent: the violent, volcanic eruption of rage is not an attempt to send a message, but simply a mute expression of the existential howl.

The paradigmatic case was recounted by Freud: a young homosexual woman who was so traumatised by seeing her father and perceiving the look he gave her as full of anger and rage, that she in an unsuccessful attempt at ending her own life climbed up a wall and threw herself onto the railroad tracks. What is crucial here is that her attempted suicide does *not* constitute a communicative attempt. It is an act that takes place beyond the web of signification, and it is precisely this sense of acting beyond meaning that positioned it as a passage to the act. Confronted with her father's desire, she was consumed by an uncontrollable anxiety and reacted in an impulsive way by identifying with the object. Thus, she fell down (Ger. *niederkommt*) like the *objet petit a*, the leftover of the signification.[23]

When the subject is destitute in this manner, it becomes purely an object. The excess of signification is precisely a surplus that is incommunicable, i.e., the object that remains beyond subjective significance. This remnant is the part of speech that the young woman identified with, and her falling onto the railroad track would place her in a position that is strictly analogous to the

---

[21] "Fortvivlelse [er] Sygdommen til Døden, denne qvalfulde Modsigelse, denne Sygdom i Selvet, evig at døe, at døe og dog ikke at døe, at døe Døden. Thi at døe betyder at det er forbi, men at døe Døden betyder at opleve det at døe; og lader dette sig eet eneste Øieblik opleve, saa er det dermed for evig at opleve det" (Kierkegaard, Sygdommen til Døden by Anti-Climacus (pseud.) [Sickness Unto Death] 1849, 12).
[22] See also Evans 1996, 137.
[23] Lacan, The Seminar of Jacques Lacan, Book X 2010, 74-75.

indestructible excess of language we associate with the trigger of desire, Lacan's small other.[24]

There is a close association between the hysterical repression that occurs as a result of the re-emergence of the fragmented body in the traumatic dissolution of fantasy in the analytic encounter and the passage. Lacan describes the story told by a young woman in his clinical practice who had married a young man against her mother's will. Becoming increasingly convinced that her in-laws and neighbours – country bumpkins, as she calls them – are plotting to "finish off this good-for-nothing city girl", she suddenly takes leave of her husband and provides the marriage with "a conclusion that had not changed in the interim", i.e., since her mother's disapproval. To Lacan, she relates the story of how her neighbour, on passing her in the hallway of their apartment building, throws an insult at her: "Sow!" Lacan then proceeds to ask "what in herself had been proffered the moment before. ...She conceded with a smile that, upon seeing the man, she had murmured ...: 'I've just been to the pork butcher's ...'".[25]

Who were her words aimed at? The girl was hard pressed to answer. Was she expressing a wish to end off her neighbour? Was it a secret message to her mother that she was executing her implied order? Lacan noted that in order to make sense of her statement, we should consider her as trapped in a dyadic relationship with her mother, i.e. in a position prior to symbolic castration and its attendant fantasies. In other words, what we have here is a case of a hysterical return of the fragmented body, where the subject "was responding once again ...to a situation that was beyond her". The difference between the homosexual woman and the city girl is therefore significant in that while the former makes no attempt to communicate, the latter sends signals even if she cannot herself make sense of her own situation in a way that makes ordinary messaging possible.

What remains crucial in Lacan's various implementations of the notion of "passage" is that they all implicate some sense of destitution. Beyond the passage to the act there is anguish and destitution, and in the third phase of the analytical process – where the analysand *passes* into analyst – the desire of the analyst is introduced in such a way as to render the subject as desiring without enjoyment, i.e. the purification of desire is achieved only through a loss of *jouissance*.[26]

---

[24] On *schema L* (figure 5.1 above) the term *a'* indicate this small other (in French *petit autre*), which is sometimes referred to as the *objet petit a*.
[25] Lacan, On a question prior to any possible treatment of psychosis 2006, 448.
[26] Žižek, The undergrowth of enjoyment 1999, 32.

When Lacan introduced the pass as a procedure to mark the end of the analysis, it was intended as formalising the analysands passage into an analytic posterior that had as its quintessential characteristic that the lessons learned from analysis could be put into language so as to be transmitted as a form of teaching. There was a clear distinction between the status gained through the pass – formally the person who had passed (*le passant*) would receive the title *Analyste de L'École* – and institutional recognition as clinical practitioner, which, in Lacan's school amounted to being awarded an A.M.E. – *Analyste Membre de L'École*.[27] The passage was not a qualification to practice clinical psychoanalysis, but merely a recognition that the analysis had reached its conclusion, and that the analysand was now in a position to articulate a set of knowledges from the analytical experience. The *passant* was a voluntary initiate into the *teaching* of psychoanalysis.

What is clear is that the movement in analysis from neurosis, through hysteria, and, finally, the passage to destitution is contingent on a subject that by experiencing a sense of alienation from one's familiar world is brought through separation and loss to a new sense of self. Alienation – the modernist feeling of being in a place where one does not, or no longer, belong – is wedded to the symptom: at this stage, the subject senses the environment as strange and not fitting to one's existence, and yet this is our world. We are, in the words of the physicists, in a universe lit up by the rays from the Big Bang, progressively enabling us to see further into the void, and yet completely in the dark with the regard to the possibility of another existence, other universes, that lie beyond the scope of one's vision.

However, a simple statistical procedure suffices to cast doubt on this *Welt Anschauung*: if space is sufficiently large to contain re-occurring constellations of matter, there are Hubble volumes – parallel universes – where our existences are lived out in tandem with us, and thus providing the possibility that with every choice we make, we are creating a wedge between our universe or universes and some universe where a different choice was made in the exact same situation. This model sustains the split performed in analysis between the analysand and the real other. Out there versions of ourselves who have made difference life choices walk around perfectly unaware of the distinction that has been made, and it is through the work of analysis that we can become aware of the division.

The sense of alienation and its association with the symptom is thus overcome through a reference to the separation that has already been effected as a consequence of the choice as it is revealed through analysis. It is here that we

---

[27] See Evans 1996, 135-136.

approach what Lacan referred to as the fantasmatic image of the fragmented body: the knowledge that is accrued through sub-atomic measuring dissolves through a double uncertainty. Werner Heisenberg pointed to measurement error and pulse duration as sources of uncertainty in recording the simultaneous rendering of more than one quantity. To this should be added uncertainty associated with the initial state of the quantum system, so-called lack of causality, since causality can only be investigated in so far at it is possible to record at least two systemic states. In other words, we cannot find causal relations that exist prior to the initial state of the system.

At this level of knowledge, Heisenberg made us aware of the limits of measurements that are partly – but not solely – due to technical considerations. It is possible to adjust the probe to pulse length in such a way that one quantity can be accurately measured. However, such adjustment would be at the detriment of accuracy with regard to other quantities. The sense in which quantities cannot be *simultaneously* measured constitutes a deviation from the expectation we inherit from classical physics. It is in *this* sense that we experience a loss: the fantasy of complete, simultaneous quantifications associated with classical physics is not replicable on the sub-atomic level: our physical world assumes the guise of fragmentation, since it is only in so far as we know a particle's position that we become blinded to its velocity.

The lack of causality associated with the uncertainty with regard to the quantum system's initial state is thus strictly analogous to the unconscious instance of the Other: it has no known cause, and yet it appears to determine every relation of the subject's unconscious. In Lacan's formulation, the unconscious is the very discourse of the Other. Here, we arrive at the sense in which the psychoanalytic experience renders the world meaningful: it enables us to limit the extinctive impulse of the drive and put into language desire as a purely structural event. It follows that, as a mathematical approach to our world, the desire of the analyst is situated in spacetime that relies on a rigorous application of Einstein's *gauge freedom* to render its analytic space.

This is where the hole argument receives its full force: as demonstration of the effect of the gauge freedom, it shows how events that are distinguishable prior to the introduction of metric and matter fields simply do not exist in certain distributions. In order to render them visible, substantivalist approaches will need to claim a variety of extensions of the fields as distinct systems, rather than as equivalent. Substantivalists thus persist in their trepidations with respect to the mechanism known as Occam's Razor: when we choose between different explanations of the same events, we should choose, all else being equal, the simpler explanation. Thus, the view that a variety of extensions are equivalent appears to be preferable to the view that they constitute distinct systems.

The literalist approach to spacetime claims that each extension constitutes a literal rendering of the manifold, and that each rendering holds the same status of literality. Against this view, non-substantivalists allow that different extensions can be located in metaphoric relations to each other, i.e., that they constitute displacements of the same substantive events and that such displacements cannot find their decidability as degrees of literality in relation to the manifold.

The sense in which the view of extensions as related by metaphor becomes an acute reminder of the passage as enabling desire as pure structure, when we consider the following scenario: if, after the hole transformation, an entity no longer passes through an event in the manifold, substantivalism would hold that the two extensions constitute different sets of physical facts. However, if this event is not observable, it would not measurable to the entity in either extension. In other words, what we are confronted with here are events of non-observables, or purely structural events.

When the analyst finally arrives at the other side of the passage, the notion that unfolds is the sense in which desire is an utterly contingent and modular notion. In its most basic formulation, desire is found in articulations of the drive. However, in so far as psychoanalysis is the study of communicative beings, it is equally imaginable that all our interaction can be distributed on a field of desire. It is here that we arrive at Plato's notion of an ideal existence relatively independently of physical matter. As Max Tegmark notes, a "mathematical structure is an abstract, immutable entity existing outside of space and time", and it is this notion of structure that Lacan was grasping with his notion of the formulae of desire.[28]

For instance, in his work on temporality, Lacan noted that "the action of structure" occur not as a lived sense of linear time, but in logical time.[29] The spacetime of Lacan's Freudian unconscious postulates a timelessness that enables allows structures to act without "supplementary tales" of probability, linear temporality or the mythology of developmental maturation. Here, the parallelism between Lacan's notion of the unconscious and modern theoretical physics agree on a key notion: they both incline towards a notion of what we should call Platonism, since Lacan's formulae and mathematics "describe the universe so

---

[28] Tegmark 2003. To Lacan, *mathemes* were a way to provide a core to psychoanalysis that could be transmitted integrally. They were introduced after a model provided by Claude Lévi-Strauss' notion of *mythemes*, which sought to capture the minimal components of myths. In much the same way *mathemes* gave to psychoanalysis a formalisation that Lacan deemed necessary in its aspiration to scientific rigour. An example of Lacan's use of algebraic symbolisation is *Schema L* (see figure 5.1 above). Cf. Evans 1996, 7-9.

[29] Lacan, Logical time and the assertion of anticipated certainty 2006, Bowie 1991, 179.

well because the universe is inherently mathematical".[30] As "all of physics is ultimately a mathematics problem", we could equally say that all of psychoanalysis is a question of adopting the appropriate formulae: "they satisfy a central criterion of objective existence: they are the same no matter who studies them".

The Other silence

At this point, we should consider the Socratic technique, as it is narrated in Plato's work, in his approach to the domain of ideas. Here, it is instructive to note how the term for the ideal, the Greek is related to what Plato considered to be eternal forms. In εἶδος, it is the image or appearance of the form that is conveyed, and this relation to vision highlights the intimate connection between knowledge and sight in Plato's thinking.

When Plato thus gave a detailed description of a republic, it was appropriately a potentiality: as the etymology of εἶδος puts us on the trace of the hypothetical εἴδω, the formation of the state in Plato's dialogue was an ideal invention.[31] To its author, the republic was as possible to engender as reality as was love: entirely plausible but beset by misunderstandings and illusions. In this state, "philosophers are kings, or the kings and princes of this world have the spirit and power of philosophy, and political greatness and wisdom meet in one, and those commoner natures who pursue either to the exclusion of the other are compelled to stand aside".[32]

In other words, the Republic of Plato was contra-factual. In the society where Socrates and Plato lived and loved, the reality was that philosophers – or so it appeared to the founders of philosophy in the Western tradition – were too rarely heard. It was as if power and reason were divorced: those who held the tools to make and execute laws and edicts were not the same as those who were most able to reason. This gap served to frustrate Socrates to the extent that we hear his cry echoed in his rhetorical strategies. Foremost of these – in the sense that it is the rhetorical device we recognise as truly in the spirit of Socrates today – is the use of irony.

What we need to be very clear about is that while satire and irony are ancient modalities and techniques, they are heralded as particularly significant devices today. An oft-cited example of their elevated status is the Russian narratologist Mikhail M. Bakhtin's work on the carnival in medieval Europe. To him, satire held a unique position in its ability to unmask tyrants, turn their absolutist world on its head, and render the slave as king, even if only for the duration of

---

[30] Tegmark 2003.
[31] Liddell, Henry George, and Robert Scott 1940.
[32] Plato, The Republic 1888, 170-171.

the Saturnalia.[33] Even today we often hear that our times "cry for satire".[34] Are these not indications of a desire for power, expressed as powerlessness? Satire is the tool of those who have little power, or at least less power than they would like, in order to ridicule and make light of those they believe hold power.

The use of wit, irony or sarcasm to expose folly articulates the very essence of what we refer to as Socratic irony. Take as an example the dialogue *Phaedrus*, where the eponymous character sets out to convince Socrates that the non-lover should be preferred to the lover, as he has been convinced by his friend Lysias. In response, Socrates asks:

> O that is noble of him! I wish that he would say the poor man rather than the rich, and the old man rather than the young one; then he would meet the case of me and of many a man; his words would be quite refreshing, and he would be a public benefactor. For my part, I do so long to hear his speech, that if you walk all the way to Megara, and when you have reached the wall come back, as Herodicus recommends, without going in, I will keep you company.[35]

Is Socrates *serious* here? Hardly: would we *reasonably* say that it is noble to prefer to non-lover to the lover? His next sentence, showing his desire to Lysias to side with the poor and old, appears more genuinely felt. These are sentiments, Socrates explains, that he and many others agree with, and holding such a view would make Lysias a philanthropist.

What is even more mysterious is the final sentence in Socrates' reply. Does he *truly* desire to hear Lysias argument for a position he doesn't seem to support, is he ironic, or does he offer to walk with Phaedrus not because of the argument, but simply because of fondness for his interlocutor? It the latter is the case, it would render his reason disingenuous: it is not because he admires Lysias' sophisms, but because of his love for Phaedrus that he will spend time with him.

Lysias, the son of the host for the setting in which the later *Republic* takes place, was a lawyer and speaker in Athens, whose access to power made Socrates appear unwieldy and out of place. It is in this context that irony becomes a device to re-gain some of the position that seems lost in the *Umwelt* of political positioning. It is a form of negation: it is as if there is a hidden understanding between the ironist and his audience that the verbatim – literal – meaning is a guise under which the true meaning resides. In our case, Socrates' estimation of Lysias as noble is the literal meaning that hides the more

---

[33] Bakhtin, Rabelais and his world 1984, 6-8; cf. 82.
[34] Rothstein 2016.
[35] Plato, Phaedrus 1892, 432.

genuine sense of his words: that Phaedrus needs to re-consider the value of Lysias' statement on love.

What is crucial is to understand what Søren Kierkegaard referred to as irony's "infinite absolute negativity", so that irony should be considered a device that as such is not directed against this or that phenomenon, human folly, or speaker, but against existence itself.[36] To the ironic subject existence itself has lost its meaning, and "reality has lost its validity". These are the reasons why Kierkegaard disapproved of Socratic irony. To the Danish 19th century philosopher, Socrates rhetoric contributed to his own death warrant: Socrates would *pretend* he didn't know, and the pretence of wanting to learn works to hide his efficacy as a teacher. In other words, Socrates work had an element of deceit to it.

The execution of Socrates, then, constitutes a victimisation of philosophy to Kierkegaard. However, he goes on to note that

> This is supposedly a tragic destiny, even if the death of Socrates isn't really tragic: the Greek state actually arrive a bit back-handed with their verdict, and they also do not derive much education from his execution, since death has no reality to Socrates. To the tragic hero, death has no validity, since to him death is truly the last struggle and the final suffering.[37]

We arrive again at an interpretative uncertainty: is Socrates' destiny merely *supposedly* tragic because it wasn't truly tragic, or because it wasn't really his destiny? Kierkegaard appears to indicate the latter interpretation: since death didn't really exist to him, Socrates cannot be said to have truly died, and therefore the tragedy is annulled when we consider Socrates' immortality.

This is where Kierkegaard draws his analogy with the figure of Christ. In their immortality – as true heroes they could not regard death as a true finitude – these icons share a domain of meaning in our imaginary: they cannot die, they remain immortal, in so far as they themselves disregarded death as the final barrier against existence. However, and this is of absolute importance to Kierkegaard, there is an insurmountable difference between the two. In order to appreciate the difference, we need to consider Plato and John as apostles:

---

[36] Kierkegaard, Om Begrebet Ironi [Concerning Irony] 1841, 272-273.

[37] "Dette er nu vistnok en tragisk Skjebne, men dog er Socrates' Død egentlig ikke tragisk; og den græske Stat kommer igrunden bagefter med sin Dødsdom, og har paa den anden Side heller ei stor Opbyggelse af Dødsstraffens Execution, thi Døden har ingen Realitet for Socrates. For den tragiske Helt har Døden Gyldighed, for ham er Døden i Sandhed den sidste Strid og den sidste Lidelse" (Kierkegaard, Om Begrebet Ironi [Concerning Irony] 1841, 286-287, author's translation).

[While] John found and immediately beheld all in Christ that he, precisely by demanding silence of himself, portray in all their objectivity, as his eyes were opened to the immediate divinity in Christ; Plato through his writing creates his Socrates, since Socrates precisely in his immediate existence was merely *negative*.[38]

The notion that irony, while a necessary device to Socrates, should be regarded as a form of negativity that expresses envy and de-validates reality itself finds its correlate in John's response: silence. In the face of a power far greater than reason, John and his Christ figure do not resort to negations but choose to hold their tongue. Is it not *here* that we find the true force of the evangelical teachings?

---

[38] "Johannes fandt og umiddelbart skuede alt det i Christus, som han netop ved at paalægge sig selv Taushed fremstiller i sin hele Objektivitet, idet hans Øie aabnedes for den umiddelbare Guddommelighed i Christus; hvorimod Plato gjennem en digterisk Virksomhed skaber sin Socrates, da Socrates netop i sin umiddelbare Existents blot var negativ" (Kierkegaard, Om Begrepet Ironi [Concerning Irony] 1841, 10, emphasis in the original).

We were looked after by a quiet fellow, a philosophy scholar in private life. The first thing he did for me was to take out his penknife and cut the boot off my foot. There are people who have a gift for tending others, and so it was with this man; even seeing him reading a book by a night-light made me feel better.

Ernst Jünger

Afterword:
Outside the rock

Amidst all the mayhem and bloody carnage in the trenches of the First World War, Ernst Jünger found solace in the company of those who loved wisdom. Receiving his first wound, Jünger takes refuge in a trench that turns out to be "the home of the great god Pain".[1] A freshman to battle, the depths of this realm makes the young soldier panic: "I lost my head completely. Ruthlessly, I barged past everyone on my path, before finally, having fallen back a few times in my haste, climbing out of the hellish crush of the trench".

Then, the next morning Jünger is put on a train to Heidelberg, and it is here that he is tended to by the young scholar on medic duty. Is it not as if we encounter the young, talented Ludwig Wittgenstein, later to become the leading light bridging the philosophy of continental Europe with that of the Anglo-American world? Wittgenstein, pulled into the domain of philosophy during his visit to study aeronautics in Manchester, had volunteered to fight for the Austro-Hungarian side. It was while serving his fatherland in the early part of the previous century that he wrote the *Tractatus Logico-Philosophicus*, which he later sent off to his mentor at Cambridge, Bertrand Russell, and which, after its publication, secured Wittgenstein a place in both continental and Anglo-American philosophical traditions.[2]

Jünger's concern is chiefly with meaning: what in the world is a young man to do to make a claim for himself in his existence? Already the year prior to the outbreak of the First World War, Jünger had run off to France to volunteer for the Foreign Legion. On his return, he signed up for duty in the Prussian army on the very first day of the war, August 1, 1914.[3] This fascination with danger, putting one's life at stake, staring into the eyes of death and mortality, typifies Jünger's project. Is it all a demonstration of youthful vigour and death-defying courage? Even Jünger is compelled to answer the call: on the train to Heidelberg, the wounded soldier peers through the windows of his carriage, and has a feeling of coming "home":

---

[1] Jünger 2004, 31. The epigraph is from ibid., 33.
[2] It does not subtract from the curiosity of this encounter that Wittgenstein were to serve again during the Second World War, but this time for the opposing side: he first volunteered as a porter in a hospital and later worked as a laboratory assistant in the UK while the war raged.
[3] Hofmann 2004, vii.

> What a beautiful country it was, and eminently worth our blood and our lives. Never before had I felt its charm so clearly. I had good and serious thoughts, and for the first time I sensed that this was more than just adventure.[4]

The sense of having something for which one would sacrifice one's life is by the same token something that makes life worth living. This duality – a cause that gives meaning to life as much as death – is here clearly assigned to the country of birth, i.e., the soldier's nation is what gives his wager meaning. It is the "beauty" of the country, combined with the reassurance that it provides a "home" for the warriors, that undergirds the potential sacrifice in battle, and it is these provisions that effects in the narrator "good and serious thoughts", and which gives him the sense that warfare goes far beyond youthful fascination with courage and comradeship.

To Ludwig Wittgenstein, philosophy was an activity that was supremely concerned with questions of *meaning*. When he distinguished between false and nonsensical renderings of meaning, the implication seems to be that meaning can be allocated to the world, even if our approach to it is shrouded in mystery. What we will discuss here is derived from this conundrum: how can Wittgenstein's argument concerning *private language* throw light on a certain notion of *non-subjectivised* meaning that we find already in Freud? And how can the aesthetic experience of poetry, and specifically the work of minimalist poet Tor Ulven, show the relation between knowledges of the rock and our mysterious and often frustrated quest for meaning in our existence?

"How do we get so much the *idea* that living beings, things can feel", asks Wittgenstein.[5] And it *is* curious that we assign emotions to other people and animals, while inanimate objects are considered to have feelings only in children's games.[6] We have somehow been taught that it is admissible – at least from a logical perspective – to transfer emotions to others, but not onto stones and plants.

Again, Wittgenstein throws doubt on whether this approach to the universe of possible carriers of emotions – what analytic philosophy would call subjects with intentional mind states – by asking us to consider the following scenario:

---

[4] Jünger 2004, 33.
[5] Wittgenstein 1963, 97 [§283].
[6] However, as Wittgenstein notes, the kinds of emotions children assign to their dolls are not of the same order, since they are circumscribed by the specificity of the game. Ibid., 97 [§282].

> Couldn't I imagine having frightful pains and turning to stone while it lasted? Well, how do I know, if I shut my eyes, whether I have not turned into a stone? And if that happened, in what sense will the stone have the pains? In what sense will they be ascribable to the stone? And why need the pain have a bearer at all here?[7]

If the I that utters the emotion can recognise its own being, we could say that there is a subject of such and such a nature that has the emotions uttered by the subject. However, this approach doesn't resolve a situation where – pace Wittgenstein – someone would say, "I am a rock in pain".

Wittgenstein resolves this conundrum by reference to the soul: "only of what behaves like a human being can one say that it *has* pains. For one has to say it of a body, or, if you like, a soul which some body *has*".[8] In other words, when Wittgenstein addresses the question of whether it is false or nonsense to say that a rock has feelings, he seeks to delineate how it is that we recognize an emotion in the first place, and only then goes on to ask how it is that we ascribe this emotion to some person or object. A rock cannot have feelings, Wittgenstein concludes since it cannot be said to have a soul (even if it is a complex question what it means to *have* a soul).[9]

Still, we cannot know for certain who it is that has an emotion. We can try to get some sense of what others feel from their facial expression, but it seems that the only relevant context in which we could say that someone experiences pain is when a statement is uttered by a first person narrator to that effect.[10] However, there are two moments that challenge such a closure to Wittgenstein. First, how can we rely on our memory to inform us correctly as to what it is like to have an emotion in the present that corresponds to our previous encounters with the same feeling? And, second, when others give expressions to their emotions, how can we be sure that they use language correctly to refer to feelings?

What Wittgenstein achieved by the private language argument was to introduce two sets of uncertainties into how we approach affects and what analytic philosophy would call mind states. When we try to ascertain our own emotions, we can never be entirely sure that we record the same feeling each time we give expression to it.[11] And when we try to infer other people's emotions, we arrive at the aporia of not knowing whether their expressions are reducible

---

[7] Ibid., 97 [§283].
[8] Ibid., 98 [§283].
[9] See ibid., 97-98 [§283-§285].
[10] Ibid., 98-99 [§285-§288].
[11] Ibid., 94-95 [§270].

to subjective feelings and of the indeterminacy of reference.[12] In other words, what we have are two sets of questions: one regards the nature of language – how it is that words, such as those we use to describe sensations, become meaningful through repetition – and one regards the question of narrative address. This latter set is what gives Wittgenstein's elaboration its designation: in so far as we can no longer trust an agent to be self-consciously consistent with regard to how it reports its own sensations, and in so far as we can ascribe emotions to agents to the extent that agents give utterance to their own feelings, we can no longer be certain who it is that has an emotion and the extent to which it is possible to claim that one is in possession of an emotion that is in our exclusive domain.

The effect is to remove emotions from subjective agents: it is as if there is a collective sensorium – a soul or spirit in Hegel's sense – that is given expression through forms of communicative addresses. It is a form of knowledge given precise description in Freud's essay (published in 1919) on "A child is being beaten": while, in the first phase, the child would gleefully claim that it has a sibling that is being beaten, in the second moment it would recognise the shameful sadism it has gotten itself involved in and turn the table around, so that it now becomes the child itself that is being beaten. The initial expression of sadism is inverted into masochism, and Freud left no doubt that both those moments were premature. It is only in the third phase that the child can arrive at the statement that leaves the address of beating open: a child – one child, any child – is being beaten.

What we need to recognise is that the second phase of this encounter never actually happened: it is a knowledge "in the Real", in the sense that it is non-subjectivised.[13] It is a similar effect that is achieved by Wittgenstein's argument: sensations do not, or do not *yet*, have a proper agent, they have yet to be subjectivised, we cannot be sure *who* it actually is that have these emotions.

What we assume is what we learn from interacting with other speakers: humans and agents that act human-like have emotions. Plants and inanimate object don't.

In his rumination of the possibility of stones having emotions – including the sense in which the speaker himself would turn *into* a stone, taking the feeling, as it were, with him into the rock – Wittgenstein concludes that for us to claim that there is a subject that is in pain, we need to ascribe to the subject something like a "soul". However, such a necessary sense of self does not clarify whether "one

---

[12] Ibid., 98-99 [§285 and §288].
[13] See Žižek, Desire : drive = truth : knowledge 2005.

can say of the stone that is has a soul and *that* is what has the pain".[14] Wittgenstein ends by asking "what has a soul, or pain, to do with a stone?"

Does it not matter whether our interlocutor is human or a rock? We could ask Arthur Schopenhauer, the great 19th century pessimist, who thought we have scant hope of experiencing happiness. Or we could pose the question to one of Schopenhauer's later students, the poet Tor Ulven, who took rocks very seriously, both as sites of existence, and as objects of meditation and knowledge.

While Schopenhauer held that "a man is never happy", Ulven added that, to Leopardi, we become happier the more illusions we harbour.[15] As all these pessimists acknowledge, the source of misery in this sense is our persistent longing for satisfaction in the face of a thirst that cannot, finally, be quenched. It is here that Ulven finds the rôle of art:

> Some of art's secret lies in that it – without properly informing us as to *how* it does so – reminds us of the impossibility of satisfying a boundless need, and that in this very impossibility lies a bitter joy: we have become separated from everything we could have had and could have been, and yet we are still capable of reflecting on it.[16]

What art can provide is a kind of solace in our failings with regard to the drive. The attitude we take with regard to this failure – what analytic philosophy refer to as our mind state – seem to matter: it is as if Wittgenstein's ethical stance returns. In his moral universe, our proper position is one to accept and endure.

To Ulven, one way to render dissatisfaction and misery beyond the immediate domain of the experiencing subject was to engage a universe that consisted of "rocks and mirrors". In a short prose poem he depicts the following scenario:

> The monument is a monument to its own forgetting and its message will remain hidden until there is no-one left to make meaning of it. It is the rock you hold in your hand, which you will never reach. Only the mirror always displays the correct time. When the rock mirrors itself, it

---

[14] Wittgenstein 1963, 97 [§283].
[15] Schopenhauer, Essays 1902, 396, Ulven, Motgift [Remedy] 1996, 85.
[16] "Noe av kunstens hemmelighet [ligger] i at den, uten at vi riktig vet det, minner oss om det umulige i å tilfredsstille et uendelig behov, og at det i selve denne umuligheten murrer en bitter glede: vi er skilt fra alt det vi kunne hatt eller vært, men vi kan tenke på det". Ibid., 90, author's translation.

is not out of vanity. The mirror betrays everything, the rock nothing. As rock and mirror is that which you most want to know.[17]

The two elements that combine to provide an outside to the experiencing, second- person subject are distinct in that they have origins that point to their difference in how they have come in to being. While the rock has existed prior to man, and is, in some sense, more fundamental than he is, the mirror is an artefact created by man, partly from material made of rocks, and clearly of a different order than the rock itself. That the artifice in some sense reflects an artefact that provides it with an origin is thus indicative of art itself. As we saw in the quote above, art's essence, in Ulven's view, is to render the conditions of our existence bearable. What we need to endure is the rock-like context of our being.

The rock itself has no message, or, to be more precise, it has no message that can be deciphered by any living being. As a monument, it is as if the rock has been formed by an instance whose design is beyond the poet's comprehension.

However, this is merely an *as if*, since the rock cannot be reached, even when considered from the vantage point of eternity. What is clear is that the mirror – the artefact made by man – betrays the rock completely: it shows all visible characteristics of the rock, and it *reveals* all matters pertaining to the rock, even when it would have been desirable not to reveal them. The ground for this betrayal is thus man's design: in our drive for knowledge (of the rock) we are sure to always impose the correct time.

Is it not here that we find the ultimate betrayal embedded in the mirroring? The rock, seemingly an agent of being mirrored (it "mirrors itself"), does not seek its own reflection in order to mull over its existence: it is its own moral bounds that shows itself to the rock. However, when the mirror is introduced to the rock, so is chronological, homogeneous time. The betrayal is thus to impose on the rock a gaze that renders the object standardised and inscribed in the domain of technicity. It has become indifferent to us.

The mystery lies in the opposition between these objects: the poet can bring the stone to our presence, and he can make the mirror present the rock, but it is only through the poem as artifice that the rock and mirror can be juxtaposed in such a manner that their *presencing* becomes within our apprehension. Already Schopenhauer noted that our fleeting glimpses of presence are insufficient to give us any kind of happiness that lasts beyond the moment. What Ulven shows in his work is nevertheless that presence is possible, even though it is rendered in art, and within the bounds of an experience of art. It is in *this* sense that Ulven is right to claim that art can provide solace: it can demonstrate the fleeting char-

---

[17] Ulven, Stein og speil: mixtum compositum. [Rock and mirror] 1995, 5.

acter of existence, while it by the same token shows how this fleetingness can be rendered as an object of artistic contemplation.

Another way of approaching the duality is to venture that the rock is catatonically *silent*: it is, in this precise sense, pure interiority, and this interior of the rock is a domain that the second person addressee of the poem can "never reach". Against the notion of a particularity that is so singular that it is incommunicable, the mirror appears to its beholder as pure exteriority: the essence – what Heidegger would refer to as *Wesen* – of the mirror is to completely render objects that are beyond it. Since the mirror doesn't have any inside its incessant communication – regarded as a visual form of "betrayal" or as endless, imitative *chatter* – has no particularism: it's a wave that has a visual or aural form that cannot, finally, be reduced to a single instance.

The particle and the wave: this is how the sub-atomic components of the universe appear to us. The uncertainty that is established on their convergence gives a distinct expression to the drive. As we thirst for ever more knowledge, that which is most sought after is the certainty that would render the particle and wave as one. At the end of the drive, there is nothing: it is emptiness itself.

As the poet explains to the addressee of the text, there is something – namely knowledge that in some way resembles the rock and the mirror – that is supremely desirable to know, and yet it is unknown. Will it ever become known? If this knowledge is anything like the rock itself – the monument that the addressee holds in his or her hand – then it will only reveal itself and become meaningful when no subjects remain to receive the truth.

What we have here is a clear rendition of a knowledge that is non-subjectivised: the poem informs us that is does exist, even if it is only hinted at and not clearly articulated. The impossible stance of this knowledge resides in that it would, at the moment when someone at the level of the addressee *did* attain it, become subjectivised, and thus no longer in the beyond of the drive, i.e., as the end or purpose of the drive itself. It is a knowledge that can only be attained at the drive's completion, which is why, in Lacan's formulation of Freud's psychoanalytic approach, the drives should be considered as death drives. It is only when we attain the symbolic possibility of outsourcing the drive that we can, as desiring subjects, be relieved of the instinctual force posed by matter itself.

The question of who it is that experiences the dissatisfaction of compulsory pursuing the drive brings us to the core of the psychoanalytic experience. In the sense that the *I* that is under the sway of some affect is a subject of discourse, we can say that for as long as the emotion has not been subjectively claimed it is as of yet not subjectivised. We don't know precisely what the feeling has as its reference, and it is not yet decided who it is that experiences the emotion.

What does it mean, then, to be in the presence of a subject that does not communicate? To Lacan, violent and seemingly irrational acts that seek to address some person or instance are crucially different from acts that are made without any attempt at communication. This distinction is found already in Freud: his arch-example of a psychotic act is that of a young homosexual woman who, after meeting her father in the street and interpreting him as being upset with her, throws herself in front of a train. Here, communication itself has stopped.[18]

Lacan noted how we seem to be rendered as speakers by some instance that eludes us by quoting from the opening of T.S. Eliot's well-known poem "The hollow men":

We are the hollow men

We are the stuffed men

Leaning together

Headpiece filled with straw. Alas![19]

Lacan points out how the poem indicates the extent to which we are always in the grip of some kind of madness: the alienation of madness shows itself in "the mad subject [that] is spoken rather than speaking", so that what we have is a subject that speaks the truth, but not on its own accord.[20] In Pascal's formulation: "Men are so necessarily mad that not to be mad would amount to another form of madness".[21]

Is it not here that we should address the question of whether finding one's own ending is necessarily an act of psychosis? If such a self-inflicted event is considered to be non-communicative, then we have begun to make an argument that the one who decides to end his existence, to bring a conclusion to his individual experience of pain, and to, in the words of Ulven, no longer be

---

[18] See Evans 1996, 137, where he recounts the case from Freud, first published in 1920. Lacan's intervention on the matter was made during his seminar on January 16, 1963. The notion of passage is discussed in further detail on page 77.
[19] Eliot 1925, 123.
[20] Lacan, The function and field of speech and language in psychoanalysis 2006, 234.
[21] Ibid., 234, Pascal 1958, 110 [§414].

the one who observes the birds, the trees and the sky, but to "become a part of all that", has made a *passage to the act*.[22]

However, should we not also consider the possibility that the poetic act can be extended to beyond the aesthetic creations of life, so that life itself – and, indeed, the very boundary that renders it possible – becomes part of the poetic universe? It is here that we find the true riddle of the boundary that constitutes the very possibility of meaning in our world: in so far as existence is made worthwhile on the grounds of some domain that goes beyond our individual experience we should remain open to the possibility that the aesthetic in itself can give meaning to life, as well as to its finality.

---

[22]
"If I was dead
now, I wouldn't
have experienced this explicit sun of
June, and it's almost immovable
green leafage, I would have been
all that. "

"Om jeg var død
nå, ville jeg ikke
ha opplevd denne junidagens
overtydelige
sol, og nesten urørlige
grønne løvverk, jeg ville vært
alt det der. "

Ulven, Samlede dikt [Collected Poems] 2001, 280, author's translation.

Bibliography

Agamben, Giorgio. *The Kingdom and the Glory.* Translated by Lorenzo Chiesa with Matteo Mandarini. Stanford, California: Stanford University Press, 2011.

Anderson, Benedict. *Imagined Communities.* London: Verso, 2006 [1983].

Aristotle. "Metaphysics." *Aristotle in 23 Volumes. Vols. 17 and 18.* Edited by Gregory R. Crane and Hugh Tredennick (translator). Perseus Digital Library. 1989. http://data.perseus.org/texts/urn:cts:greekLit:tlg0086.tlg025 (accessed June 1, 2016).

Austin, John Langshaw. *How to do things with words.* London: Oxford University Press, 1962.

Bakhtin, Mikhail M. "Epic and novel." In *The Dialogic Imagination*, edited by Michael Holquist, translated by Caryl Emerson and Michael Holquist, 3-40. Austin, Texas: University of Texas Press, 1981.

—. *Rabelais and his world.* Bloomington, Indiana: Indiana University Press, 1984.

Bataille, George. *Visions of Excess.* Edited by Allan Stoekl with Carl R. Lovitt and Donald M. Leslie Jr. Minneapolis: University of Minnesota Press, 1985.

Benjamin, Walter. "Theses on the philosophy of history [On the concept of history]." In *Illuminations*, edited by Hannah Arendt, translated by Harry Zohn, 253-264. New York: Schocken, 1969 [1940].

Berger, John. *About Looking.* New York: Bloomsbury, 2009.

Berkeley, George. *A Treatise Concerning the Principles of Human Knowledge.* Philadelphia: J.B. Lippincott & Co., 1874.

Borges, Jorge Luis. *The Book of Imaginary Beings.* Translated by Norman Thomas di Giovanni. London: Random House, 2002.

Bourdieu, Pierre. "The field of cultural production, or: the economic world reversed." In *The Field of Cultural Production*, edited by Randal Johnson, 29-73. Cambridge: Polity, 1993.

Bourne, Daniel. "A conversation with Jorge Luis Borges." *Artful Dodge, Vol. 2, no. 2.* 1980. http://artfuldodge.sites.wooster.edu/content/jorge-luis-borges (accessed May 27, 2016).

Bowie, Malcolm. *Lacan.* London: Fontana Press, 1991.

Bull, Malcolm. "Decline of decacence." *New Left Review*, July-August 2015: 83-102.

Debord, Guy. *Society of the Spectacle.* Detroit: Black & Red, 1983 [1967].

Deleuze, Gilles. *Foucault.* Translated by Paul Bove. London: Continuum, 2006.

Derrida, Jacques. "Before the Law." In *Acts of Literature*, edited by Derek Attridge, translated by Avital Ronell, 183-220. London: Routledge, 1992.

—. "The law of genre." *Critical Inquiry*, 1980: 55-81.

—. "Plato's pharmacy." In *Dissemination*, translated by Barbara Johnson, 63-171. Chicago: University of Chicago Press, 1981.

Diogenes Laertius. *Lives of Eminent Philosophers.* Translated by Robert Drew Hicks. Vol. 2. London: W. Heinemann, 1925.

Dryden, John. "The author's apology for heroic poetry and poetic licence." In *Essays of John Dryden, vol. 1*, translated by W. P. Ker, 178-190. London: Clarendon Press, 1900 [1677].

Einstein, Albert. "My theory." *The Times*, November 1919: 41-43.

Eliasson, Olafur. *The Weather Project. Installation: Monofrequency lights, projection foil, haze machines, mirror foil, aluminium, scaffolding.* 22,7 m x 22,3 m x 155,44 m. Turbine Hall at Tate Modern, London, 2003.

Eliot, Thomas Sterns. *Poems: 1909--1925*. London: Faber & Gwyer, 1925.

Elster, Jon. *Solomonic Judgements: studies in the limitations of rationality.* Cambridge: Kluwer, 1989.

Evans, Dylan. *An Introductory Dictionary of Lacanian Psychoanalysis.* London: Routledge, 1996.

Frankl, Viktor. *Man's Search for Meaning.* Translated by Ilse Lasch. Boston, Mass.: Simon & Schuster, 1992.

Freud, Sigmund. ""A child is being beaten': a contribution to the study of the origin of sexual perversions." In *The Standard Edition of the Complete Psychological Works of Sigmund Freud, vol. XVII.* London: Hogarth Press, 1919.

—. *Moses and Monotheism.* Translated by Katherine Jones. Letchworth, Hertfordshire: Institute of Psycho-analysis, 1939.

—. *Three Contributions to the Theory of Sex.* 4th ed. Translated by A.A. Brill. New York and Washington: Nervous and Mental Disease Publishing Co., 1930.

—. *Totem and Taboo.* Translated by A.A. Brill. New York: Moffat, Yard and Company, 1918.

Gall, Robert S. "Living on (happily) ever after: Derrida, philosophy and the comic." *Philosophy Today*, 1994: 167-180.

Gudmundsson, Sigurður. *Come back Muse. Oil paint on hammered messing, artificial tree, wood.* 105 cm x 72 cm x 53 cm / 133 cm x 73 cm x 53 cm. Galerie van Gelder, Amsterdam. 2013.

Guénard, Florent, and Landemore, Hélène. "'When the lottery is fairer than rational choice.' Interview with Jon Elster." *La Vie des idées.* 26 November 2008. http://www.laviedesidees.fr/IMG/pdf/20081119_Elster_en.pdf (accessed June 3, 2016).

Hegel, Georg Wilhelm Friedrich. *Lectures on the Philosophy of History.* Translated by John Sibree. London: Bell, 1914.

—. *Vorlesungen über die Ästhetik.* Vol. 3. Berlin: Duncker und Humblot, 1838.

Heidegger, Martin. *Basic Writings.* Edited by David Farrell Krell. London: Routledge, 2008.

—. "Building dwelling thinking." In *Basic Writings*, edited by David Farrell Krell, 243-255. London: Routledge, 2008.

—. *Discourse on Thinking.* Translated by John M. Anderson and E. Hans Freund. New York: Harper & Row, 1966.

—. *Kant und das Problem der Metaphysik.* Frankfurt am Main: Vittorio Klostermann, 1991.

—. "Letter on Humanism." In *Basic Writings*, edited by David Farrell Krell, 147-181. London: Routledge, 2008.

—. "The origin of the work of art." In *Basic Writings*, edited by David Farrell Krell, 89-139. London: Routledge, 2008.

—. "What is metaphysics?" In *Basic Writings*, edited by David Farrell Krell, 45-57. London: Routledge, 2008.

Heisenberg, Werner. "Über den anschaulichen Inhalt der quantentheoretischen Kinematik und Mechanik [The actual content of quantum theoretical kinematics and mechanics]." *Zeitschrift für Physik*, 1927: 172-198.

Heraclitus. *The Fragments of the Work of Heraclitus of Ephesus on Nature*. Translated by G.T.W. Patrick. Baltimore: N. Murray, 1889.

Hilgevoord, Jan, and Jos Uffink. "The uncertainty principle." *Stanford Encyclopedia of Philosophy*. 2006. http://plato.stanford.edu/entries/qt-uncertainty/ (accessed June 8, 2016).

Hofmann, Michael. "Introduction." In *Storm of Steel*, by Ernst Jünger, translated by Michael Hofmann, vii–xxii. London: Penguin, 2004.

Horace. "Ars Poetica, or epistle to the Pisos." In *Satires. Epistles. The Art of Poetry*, translated by H. Rushton Fairclough. Cambridge, Mass.: Harvard University Press, 1926.

Janko, Richard. "Empedocles, On Nature I 233-264: a new reconstruction of P. Strasb. gr. Inv. 1665-6." *Zeitschrift für Papyrologie und Epigraphik*, 2005: 1–25.

Jeffries, Stuart. "I got dangerously close to Johnny." *The Guardian*. 15 August 2008. https://www.theguardian.com/film/2008/aug/15/mikeleigh (accessed June 8, 2016).

Johnson, Barbara. "Introduction." In *Dissemination*, translated by Barbara Johnson, vii–xxxiii. Chicago: University of Chicago Press, 1981.

Jünger, Ernst. *Storm of Steel*. Translated by Michael Hofmann. London: Penguin, 2004.

Kandellmarch, Jonathan. "Imre Kertesz, Nobel laureate who survived Holocaust, dies at 86." 1 April 2016. http://www.nytimes.com/2016/04/01/world/europe/imre-kertesz-dies.html (accessed June 6, 2016).

Kant, Immanuel. *The Critique of Pure Reason*. Translated by John Miller Dow Meiklejohn. New York: Willey Book Co., 1899.

Kasparov, Garry. "The chess master and the computer. Review of Diego Rasskin-Gutman, Chess Metaphors: artificial intelligence and the human mind." 11 February 2010. http://www.nybooks.com/articles/2010/02/11/the-chess-master-and-the-computer/ (accessed June 3, 2016).

Kierkegaard, Søren. *Om Begrepet Ironi [Concerning Irony]*. Copenhagen: P.G. Philipsens Forlag, 1841.

—. *Sygdommen til Døden by Anti-Climacus (pseud.) [Sickness Unto Death]*. Copenhagen: C. A. Reitzels Forlag, 1849.

Kittang, Atle. *Sigmund Freud*. Oslo: Gyldendal, 1997.

Knausgård, Karl Ove. *Min kamp. 6 vols*. Oslo: Oktober, 2007-2011.

Kunze, Donald. "middle voice and topical invention." 1988. http://art3idea.psu.edu/locus/middle_voice.pdf (accessed June 3, 2016).

Lacan, Jacques. "Aggressiveness in psychoanalysis." In *Écrits*, translated by Bruce Fink, 82–101. New York: W.W. Norton & Co., 2006.

—. "Desire and the interpretation of desire in Hamlet." In *Literature and Psychoanalysis*, edited by Shoshana Felman, 11–52. London: Johns Hopkins University Press, 1982.

—. *Écrits*. Translated by Bruce Fink. New York: W.W. Norton & Co., 2006.

—. "Logical time and the assertion of anticipated certainty." In *Écrits*, translated by Bruce Fink, 161–175. New York: W.W. Norton & Co., 2006.

—. "On a question prior to any possible treatment of psychosis." In *Écrits*, translated by Bruce Fink, 445–488. New York: W.W. Norton & Co., 2006.

—. "Seminar on 'The purloined letter'." In *Écrits*, translated by Bruce Fink, 6–48. New York: W.W. Norton & Co., 2006.

—. "The direction of the treatment and the principles of its power." In *Écrits*, translated by Bruce Fink, 489–542. New York: W.W. Norton & Co., 2006.

—. *The Four Fundamental Concepts of Psycho-Analysis*. New York: W.W. Norton & Co., 1977.

—. "The function and field of speech and language in psychoanalysis." In *Écrits*, translated by Bruce Fink, 197–268. New York: W.W. Norton & Co., 2006.

—. "The instance of the letter in the unconscious, or reason since Freud." In *Écrits*, translated by Bruce Fink, 412–441. New York: W.W. Norton & Co., 2006.

—. *The Seminar of Jacques Lacan, Book X*. Translated by Cormac Gallagher. 2010.

Lange, Marc. "Did Einstein really believe that principle theories are explanatorily powerless?" *Perspectives on Science*, 2014: 449–463.

Laurent, Eric. "The Purloined Letter and the Tao of the psychoanalyst." In *The Later Lacan*, edited by Véronique Voruz and Bogdan Wolf, 25–52. Albany, New York: State University of New York Press, 2007.

Naked. Film. Directed by Mike Leigh. Produced by Channel Four. 1993.

Lévi-Strauss, Claude. "The structural study of myth." *The Journal of American Folklore*, 1955, 68.270 ed.: 428–444.

Liddell, Henry George, and Robert Scott. *A Greek-English Lexicon*. Edited by Gregory R. Crane. Perseus Digital Library. 1940. http://perseus.uchicago.edu/ (accessed August 29, 2015).

Miłosz, Czesław. *Facing the River*. Hopewell, New Jersey: Ecco Press, 1995.

Nabokov, Vladimir. *Speak, Memory*. London: Penguin, 2000.

Nietzsche, Friedrich. *The Gay Science*. Translated by Walter Kaufmann. New York: Random House, 1974.

Norton, John D. "The hole argument." Stanford Encyclopedia of Philosophy. 2015. http://plato.stanford.edu/entries/spacetime-holearg/ (accessed June 8, 2016).

O'Sullivan, Simon. "Definition: 'fold'." 2005. http://simonosullivan.net/articles/deleuze-dictionary.pdf (accessed May 27, 2016).

Parmenides. "On nature." In *Early Greek Philosophy*, edited by John Burnet, translated by John Burnet, 196–203. London: A. and C. Black, 1908.

Pascal, Blaise. *Pascal's Pensées*. Translated by William Finlayson Trotter. New York: E.P. Dutton, 1958.

Plato. *Cratylus*. Vol. 1, in *The Dialogues of Plato in Five Volumes*, translated by Benjamin Jowett, 323–389. Oxford: Clarendon Press, 1892.

—. *Ion.* Vol. 1, in *The Dialogues of Plato in Five Volumes*, translated by Benjamin Jowett, 497–511. Oxford: Clarendon Press, 1892.

—. *Phaedrus.* Vol. 1, in *The Dialogues of Plato in Five Volumes*, translated by Benjamin Jowett, 431–489. Oxford: Clarendon Press, 1892.

—. "Protagoras." 1967. http://data.perseus.org/texts/urn:cts:greekLit:tlg0059.tlg022 (accessed June 3, 2016).

—. "Symposium." 1925. http://data.perseus.org/texts/urn:cts:greekLit:tlg0059.tlg011 (accessed June 10, 2016).

—. *The Republic.* Vol. 3, in *The Dialogues of Plato in Five Volumes*, translated by Benjamin Jowett. Oxford: Clarendon Press, 1888.

Pliny the Elder. *The Natural History.* Translated by John Bostock and H.T. Riley. Vol. 5. London: Henry G. Bohn, 1856.

Plutarch. *Of curiosity [De curiositate].* Vol. 2, in *Plutarch's Essays*, edited by William W. Goodwin, translated by Maurice Wheeler, 424– 445. Boston: Little, Brown, 1909.

Rank, Otto. *Der Mythus von der Geburt des Helden.* Leipzig: Franz Deuticke, 1909.

Rilke, Rainer Maria. *Poems.* New York: Tobias A. Wright, 1918.

Rothstein, Klaus. "Tida ropar på satire – til fånyttes [Our times are crying out for satire – to no avail]." *Prosa*, no. 22.2 (2016).

Saussure, Ferdinand de. *Course in General Linguistics.* London: Duckworth, 1983.

Schellekens, Elisabeth. "Conceptual art." Stanford Encyclopedia of Philosophy. 2014. url: http://plato.stanford.edu/entries/conceptual-art/ (accessed June 7, 2016).

Schirmacher, Wolfgang. "Art(ificial) perception: Nietzsche and culture after nihilism." *Poiesis*, 1999: 4–8.

Schopenhauer, Arthur. *Essays.* Translated by Mrs. Rudolf Dircks. London: Walter Scott Pub. Co., 1897.

—. *Essays.* Translated by T. Bailey Saunders. New York: Boni & Liveright, 1902.

Taxi Driver. Film. Directed by Martin Scorsese. Produced by Columbia. 1976.

Skeat, Walter W. *An Etymological Dictionary of the English Language.* London: Clarendon Press, 1888.

Stevens, Alexandre. "Embarrasment, inhibition, and repetition." In *The Later Lacan*, edited by Véronique Voruz and Bogdan Wolf, 147– 157. Albany, New York: State University of New York Press, 2007.

Tegmark, Max. "Parallel universes." *Scientific American*, 2003.

Trausil, Hans. "Introduction." In *Poems*, by Rainer Maria Rilke, translated by Jessie Lemont, xiii–xxxvi. New York: Tobias A. Wright, 1918.

Ulven, Tor. *Avløsning (Roman) [Succession (Novel)].* Oslo: Gydendal, 1993.

—. *Essays.* Oslo: Gyldendal, 1997.

—. "Motgift [Remedy]." 1996. http://www.oktober. no/nor/content/download/4718/16966/version/1/file/Samtale+med+ Tor + Ulven.pdf (accessed February 12, 2004).

—. *Samlede dikt [Collected Poems].* Oslo: Gyldendal, 2001.

—. *Stein og speil: mixtum compositum. [Rock and mirror].* Oslo: Gyldendal, 1995.

Voruz, Véronique. "A Lacanian reading of Dora." In *The Later Lacan*, edited by Véronique Voruz and Bogdan Wolf, 158–179. Albany, New York: State University of New York Press, 2007.

—, and Bogdan Wolf, eds. *The Later Lacan*. Albany, New York: State University of New York Press, 2007.

Wiener, Jan. "Under the volcano: varieties of anger and their transformation." In *Journal of Analytic Psychology*, 493–508. 1998.

Wittgenstein, Ludwig. *Philosophical Investigations*. Translated by G.E.M. Anscombe. Oxford, 1963.

Žižek, Slavoj. "Da Capo senza Fine." In *Contingency, Hegemony, Universality*, edited by Ernesto Laclau and Slavoj Žižek Judith Butler, 213– 262. London, 2000.

—. "Desire : drive = truth : knowledge." 2005. http://www.lacan.com/zizek-desire.htm (accessed October 30, 2017).

—. "Holding the place." In *Contingency, Hegemony, Universality*, edited by Ernesto Laclau and Slavoj Žižek Judith Butler, 308–329. London: Verso, 2000.

—. "Is it possible to traverse the fantasy in cyberspace?" In *The Žižek Reader*, edited by Elizabeth and Edmund Wright Wright, 104–124. Oxford: Blackwell, 1999.

—. "The undergrowth of enjoyment." In *The Žižek Reader*, edited by Elizabeth and Edmund Wright Wright, 11–36. Oxford: Blackwell, 1999.

Index

A

aha-Erlebnis, 5, 45
alienation, 30, 31, 82, 89, 94, 110
Anderson, Benedict, xix, 23, 32, 33, 34, 113, 114
Aristotle, 17, 18, 63, 113

B

Bakhtin, Mikhail M., 23, 33, 34, 97, 98, 113
Barry, Robert, xx, 78
Being, xiv, xv, xix, 10, 13, 14, 26, 27, 30, 37, 38, 39, 40, 51, 56, 57, 59
Benjamin, Walter, 23, 32, 33, 35, 113, 116, 117
Berger, John, 61, 62, 113
Berkeley, George, 27, 113
Borges, Jorge Luis, 2, 51, 52, 113
Bourdieu, Pierre, 68, 113
Brecht, Bertolt, 64

C

Christ, xx, 33, 82, 99, 100
chronotope, 23
commodity, 32, 35, 40
concept, xx, 75, 76, 78, 79, 117
cyclical, 31, 32, 34, 35, 40

D

Dasein, 14, 37, 38, 57
Debord, Guy, xix, 25, 31, 32, 34, 35, 40, 113

Derrida, Jacques, 2, 24, 50, 51, 52, 53, 54, 55, 56, 113, 114
desire, xx, 2, 10, 13, 15, 24, 25, 37, 46, 47, 48, 49, 50, 54, 55, 70, 71, 82, 88, 89, 90, 92, 93, 95, 96, 98, 116, 118
despair, 92
Diogenes Laertius, 17, 18, 113
drive, xv, xvi, xx, xxi, 15, 19, 37, 50, 79, 86, 95, 96, 106, 107, 108, 109, 118
Dryden, John, xix, 65, 67, 68, 114

E

Einstein, Albert, xvii, 83, 85, 86, 95, 114, 116
Eliasson, Olafur, 76, 114
Empedocles, xviii, 14, 16, 17, 18, 19, 39, 115
epoch, xv, xvi, 23

F

forgetting, xix, 53, 56, 57, 58, 59, 60, 107
Frankl, Victor, 43, 44, 59, 114
Freud, Anna, 13, 28, 46
Freud, Sigmund, xx, 5, 6, 7, 8, 11, 12, 13, 15, 19, 24, 28, 30, 43, 45, 46, 61, 89, 90, 92, 104, 106, 109, 110, 114, 115, 116

G

gaze, 27, 28, 58, 61, 74, 79, 90, 108
Giacometti, Alberto, 73, 79, 80
gift, 14, 50, 53, 54, 101

groundless ground, 37, 41
Gudmundsson, Sigurður, 77, 78, 114

H

Heidegger, Martin, xiv, xv, xix, 11, 12, 14, 16, 17, 36, 37, 38, 39, 40, 41, 50, 53, 57, 58, 59, 67, 75, 109, 114
Heisenberg, Werner, xvi, xvii, 81, 84, 85, 86, 95, 115
Heraclitus, xix, 4, 5, 6, 7, 8, 9, 12, 15, 16, 18, 25, 115
hole argument, 86, 87, 88, 95, 116
Horace, 18, 19, 20, 115
hyperperception, xix, 58, 59

I

indeterminacy, xiii, 2, 14, 38, 52, 53, 106

J

Jünger, Ernst, 103, 104, 115

K

Kant, Immanuel, 36, 38, 39, 40, 57, 114, 115
Kasparov, Garry, 36, 115
Kertész, Imre, 59
Kierkegaard, Søren, 82, 92, 99, 100, 115
Knausgård, Karl Ove, 43, 115

L

Lacan, Jacques, xvii, 1, 10, 11, 12, 13, 14, 15, 17, 24, 25, 27, 28, 29, 30, 31, 39, 45, 46, 47, 48, 49, 50, 54, 57, 71, 78, 82, 83, 84, 88, 90, 91, 92, 93, 94, 95, 96, 109, 110, 113, 115, 116, 117, 118
linear, 2, 32, 35, 40, 96
love, xix, 10, 11, 12, 15, 16, 89, 90, 97, 98, 99

M

Miłosz, Czesław, xx, 67, 69, 116
multiverse, 81, 82, 83

N

Naked (film), 81, 116
negation, xx, 62, 63, 66, 98
Nietzsche, Friedrich, 17, 58, 59, 116, 117
non-subjectivised, xx, 104, 106, 109

O

objectivity, xx, 26, 30, 34, 38, 45, 82, 97, 100
Occam's Razor, 95
ontology, xvii, 10, 51
Other, xix, 10, 11, 12, 15, 26, 27, 29, 30, 31, 45, 46, 47, 48, 49, 56, 57, 82, 83, 89, 91, 95, 97

P

pain, 89, 105, 106, 110
Parmenides, xix, 9, 10, 11, 12, 16, 18, 116
particular, xv, xx, 3, 10, 35, 45, 47, 57, 58, 63, 64, 65, 68, 71, 73, 75, 91
passage, xiv, xvii, xx, 1, 52, 81, 88, 91, 92, 93, 94, 96, 110, 111
    passage to the act, 1, 81, 88, 91, 92, 93, 111
passe, 88

Index

phallic function, xix, 2, 10, 11, 15, 29, 47, 48, 49, 50, 88
   Father, 6, 10, 11, 12, 24, 29, 46, 47, 54
   phallus, xvi, 9, 11, 14
Plato, xvi, xvii, xix, xx, 3, 4, 9, 17, 20, 44, 53, 54, 55, 56, 62, 63, 64, 65, 66, 67, 96, 97, 98, 99, 100, 113, 116, 117
   Ion, 3, 4, 20, 63, 117
   Phaedrus, 53, 55, 98, 99, 117
   The Republic, 4, 20, 21, 55, 63, 67, 97, 98, 117
praising, 32, 41
presencing, 50, 58, 59, 70, 108
principle theories, 85, 116

R

Rank, Otto, 6, 7, 117
rationality, xv, 36, 37, 43, 114
   calculative thinking, xv
   homo oeconomicus, 36
   meditative thinking, xv, xix
   rational choice, 36, 37, 114
Real, 14, 17, 48, 49, 106
releasement (*Gelassenheit*), xix

S

Saussure, Ferdinand de, 52, 70, 71, 77, 78, 117
Schirmacher, Wolfgang, xix, 57, 58, 59, 117
Schopenhauer, Arthur, xvi, 56, 57, 107, 108, 117
separation, 15, 16, 24, 30, 48, 79, 82, 83, 89, 90, 94

sexuation, xx, 29, 49, 88
   sexual, 11, 14, 17, 49, 89, 90, 114
spacetime, xvii, 81, 86, 87, 95, 96, 116
subjective, 12, 25, 26, 30, 45, 46, 48, 50, 57, 58, 92, 106
subjectivity, 12, 29, 56, 57
   barred subject, 12, 13, 14, 30, 78, 91
   ek-centric, 13, 50
   ek-sistence, 14
   ex-static, 50
   Schema L, 83, 93
   social *I*, 29, 30

T

Taxi Driver (film), 2, 117
technology, xvi, 53, 54, 58
torus, 13, 14, 39
transference, 45, 46
transversal, xvi, 33, 82, 90, 91

U

Ulven, Tor, xiii, xviii, xx, xxi, 14, 67, 71, 72, 73, 74, 79, 104, 107, 108, 110, 111, 117
uncertainty, xvi, 85, 86, 95, 99, 109, 115

W

Wittgenstein, Ludwig, xiii, xiv, xx, 103, 104, 105, 106, 107, 118
   private language, xiv, xx, 104, 105

www.ingramcontent.com/pod-product-compliance
Lightning Source LLC
Chambersburg PA
CBHW050556300426
44112CB00013B/1941